Dear Clare,
I hope

tr

Be...
x

Dedicated to Luke whose presence made me believe my dreams could come true and my Mum for inspiring me to write.

For Anna and Zoe for supporting me in my every endeavour.

READER REVIEWS

Emma Taylor:

> *"I finished this with tears in my eyes and a feeling of renewed appreciation of life, love and the journey we all take. Becca provides a beautifully honest account of world travel, love, mental health struggles and wonderful moments that will have you laughing, crying and gasping."*

Clare Pennington:

> *"Very well written, loved reading about Manic Mick and PMT Polly's travels and amazing adventures. So good I read it all the same day it was delivered"*

Amazon Customer:

"Really loved this book. Laugh aloud funny, heartfelt and honest."

Travelling Light & Dark:

One year around the world with Manic Mick & PMT Polly.

"The path is longer than the one you take."

These are the last words I spoke in a past life. I was regressed back by a hypnotherapist. *

*(I'm still trying to work out what it means.)

INTRODUCTION

I was working at my desk when my colleague Dani said her son had been inconsolably upset that morning. Why? They had to leave Ibiza for Lincolnshire a few days earlier and Dani told him "that's the way the world works George, you work hard all year for your 2-week holiday".

I no longer felt like this was the truth for me. I was planning to hand in my notice and travel the world full time for 1 year.

This book is written to inspire your inner (inconsolable) child to encourage you to follow your long-held dream.

It is also written for Luke and I, so we can remember our year away with all its light and darkness.

BECCA MEETS LUKE

Mick & Polly aren't our real names.

When I first heard about 'Manic Mick' I was apprehensive. I wondered if he was a character Luke made up in order to avoid responsibility for his bad behavior. Once I had heard myself be called 'PMT Polly' I understood. It was his way to cope with his fractured personality. I can't help being irate and emotional a few days before my period (cue Polly) anymore than he can help waking up as another person; like 'Moaning Morris' or 'Depressive Dan'. Luke has had mental health problems since a head injury in 2006. He was attacked by a man with a baseball bat and spent over a month in a coma. When we met a decade later we needed each other to move on to the next chapter of our lives. Six months prior, I had emerged from a destructive relationship into a resolution that my life was my own. I was holding on to it tightly, I knew how special it was to have the rest of my life in my hands but I didn't know what I wanted to do with it. I didn't want my flat, my job, my alone-ness, sadness, stress or anxiety. The giant world map I had just bought gave me some clue of where I thought I might go. 'There', I wanted to go into the map, but it was too big, I couldn't look directly at the world. I wasn't ready.

I met Luke a few days later, on a dating app called 'Plenty of Fish'. His picture was of him in Thailand, topless with a cowboy hat on. I said I was a non-smoker. I always loved travelling, experiencing new things and although I made the most of my time alone, I was looking for true love. Each of our dates revealed a little more of his incredible story. The story which I will weave into this book. Our first date chatter was about a hypothetical route we would take around the world. I said "I have family in Canada," he said, "ok we'll go there first".

I looked into his eyes, dark, deep, and vulnerable. He insisted on buying us the second round of drinks as well as the first. We were in a bubble, in a dark corner of a pub in Lincoln and we both felt a big spark. The next day, I invited him along to my walking group. I was doing things that lit me up and I loved sharing that with Luke. I was late to the walk meet and saw him checking out his hair as I pulled up. The whole group was waiting for me in the middle of nowhere. There was probably a more convenient walk to join but I hadn't worked out how to use 'The Ramblers' guidebook. He talked a lot, and then at the pub afterwards he really talked a load more, but I saw past it, my yoga practice had taught me to trust my intuition and despite Luke repeating the same story about 'Pirate' juice, a drink he had 'created' in Thailand from various cordials, I let it go, I enjoyed the walk and I was buzzing. I sat and spoke to a young girl who told me a 'friend' of hers had locked her in a house and broke her arm. It reminded me of what I had escaped from. Luke, although clearly mad was no harm, he was funny, loving and caring and an adventurer like me. When we got lost on the way home we realised that although we both loved travelling we had zero sense of direction between us.

Luke said he had been sick earlier that day and almost wasn't going to come on the walk. He managed to bring himself round by having a cold bath. The prospect of a first kiss seemed a bit gross, but we decided to go for it anyway, an incredible first kiss. Each sat in our own seat, in my car, still lost, but we'd found each other's tongues. After just two dates we were exchanging possibly contagious saliva. Anytime one of us coughs nowadays we go straight in for a kiss to bring back the memories of our first smooch. Our willingness to infect the other with whatever we may be suffering from bonds us together. We are just another couple who have weird favourite 'things to do', if you are single then I know how sickened you might feel, I've been there. I was always the wino third wheel, hearing about how Lauren & Rogier love Strawberry Ribena, or watching Anna & Scott make cheese and biscuits together. Each time I felt jealousy rising I managed to turn it round and say to myself, you will have a favourite thing with someone one day. Now Luke and I like sweet & salty popcorn and each other's colds.

When I met Luke's family on the Sunday of that week, he sneezed his dinner onto his Nan's wall in front of me and his little nephew; Josh. Naturally we all bonded for life over possibly the most hilarious thing that's ever happened at dinner. My own Nannie's roast dinners were legendary. There were people at her funeral who were there to show respect for her marvelous feasts. I missed Nannie, her food, the care she took of me, but now I had been invited into Luke's family, it felt good to have his Nan; Dawny, care for us.

The next week Luke & I arranged to meet by the river in Farndon near Newark. I wore a long red evening gown and took along my microphone to use as a prop while serenading Luke with 'Linger' by the Cranberries! When it came to it though I got stage fright so we trekked so far into some long grass for me to find the 'right spot' that we were bitten to pieces by mosquitos. Even Bruiser, Luke's dog who was running around the car park as I pulled up was getting frustrated. Later as we waited for our chicken skewers to cook on the barbeque Luke did some Yoga moves, including a head stand which caused his top to fall down and expose his 6 pack. Safe to say I fell in love, I told him I would never get bored of watching him practice yoga. After the singing and dinner Luke opened up to me that he had been off work for a few months due to mental health problems. He worked as a Peer Support Worker bridging the gap between patient and doctor, for people struggling with their own mental health at Nottinghamshire Healthcare trust, a part of the NHS.

Date after date led us to Friday night, Luke wanted to show the other side of himself, he took me to a house party where we stayed up all night taking party drugs. He was testing me. He had said a few nights before that he wanted a girlfriend to stop him taking drugs, I said I would never tell him what to do. That was up to him. I got on really well with all his friends and spent the night singing old country songs to a travelling girl called Claire, who introduced herself to me by asking for £20 for a palm reading. I also smoked all of the host's menthol cigarettes.

I was beginning to see the antics borne from Luke's Bi-polar personality. One, a picnic loving yogi in hand sewn pants from Thailand, the other, a weed smoking all night raver. I was (mostly) ecstatic to be taken for the ride.

Over the next twelve months we gave each other the confidence to finally follow our dream of travelling. We conquered the impossibilities of quitting 10-year-long careers and cut ties with every direct debit. Just a few months into our relationship I gave up my flat and moved in with a friend, in order to save money for our trip.

* * *

Luke and I later moved in together, to learn how to be with each other full-time. It was not plain sailing. Luke had never lived with a woman long term before. We were both very independent. I annoyed him but he didn't say anything as he was being polite. Politeness would give way to arguments and we 'had everything out' that had annoyed each other thus far. Luckily, each time we thought something might break us, we came out stronger than before. Looking back, that time in his flat seemed ideal, we had a dog, I would walk barefoot around the fields with Bruiser while Luke cooked healthy tea. We didn't have a table, so for special occasions we would eat at the ironing board and as a real treat Luke would bring a bottle of Rosé from the shop just 2 minutes away. His Nan even cleaned the house and did our laundry! I brought with me the world map so we had bigger plans. We would be venturing into the unknown together, we were excited that finally we had found another person to share our dream of travel with. Each Sunday night we wrote out a to-do list for the week, bought loads of stuff online, like sleeping bag liners, mosquito nets and locks for our bags. None of which we took with us as in the end we decided to travel light.

Luke supported me through starting my own Social Media Management business and bringing an end to a stressful career in advertising sales. I bought a yellow Beetle for about £400. The seller lived in the middle of nowhere and the car only started with jump leads but I had wanted this colour Beetle for as long as I could remember. Luke bartered him down for me from about £600. I was following Luke home from North-Yorkshire with no sat nav, no insurance or clue about whether the old banger would make the journey when Luke sped off and left me! Apparently, I was 'taking too long'. I somehow got back to Newark, thrilled with my new 2 litre 'Bug', the first car I've ever owned, having had company cars up until then. Dreams were coming true, anything seemed possible. Questionable decisions were becoming my norm after years of 'doing the right thing'. I started to wear my walking boots more with long floaty dresses and shaved half my head. I gave up all the designer heels, tight dresses and the 'tits & teeth' of sales.

We joined the National Trust and every weekend was spent at a beautiful new location. I wanted to go to a Tibetan monastery in Scotland for my 31st birthday. Luke booked that for us plus a 2 nights stay in an ancient Scottish castle in Edinburgh. We did a yoga course together at the monastery in an amazing week of living as a monk and a princess. The sign of things to come. Despite protesting that I would rather live simply on our world trip, I was treated to a helicopter ride, a trip on a yacht and a 14,000ft skydive. The jump from a plane was the only situation free from stress and near complete disaster. We have travelled through light, carefree days and some very dark days.

While testing out our survival skills we got lost in a Nottingham country park in December. I had bought Luke an eco-stove (Kelly Kettle), which we wanted to try out but all we had to burn was some icy leaves and a spare tampon. We tried for hours to make a fire in the base of the stove but failed. The sun went down, we were left walking around the deserted gardens looking for Luke's car in the pitch black. I thought I could see its outline. I told Luke to press the unlock button on his key fob and... thankfully... the shape we were looking at was our ride home! We had narrowly avoided freezing to death. Our mantra was 'getting lost is the adventure' and we really had to lose the stress surrounding being lost. We learnt we could choose to be stressed, or we could be amused, this helped us through many more times of not having a clue where we were.

As it turned out, getting lost was the least of our problems during our year to come.

PLANNING THE TRIP

From 1st August 2016, (our first date), to 1st August 2017, (when we left the UK), we worked hard on pre-trip preparation.

I had a book called 'The World', from Lonely Planet and we stuck a post-it note on every place we intended to visit. The route didn't differ much from what we had discussed on our first date. Luke added Guatemala and I insisted on some trekking in Nepal. We planned a short time in America as we anticipated the U.S. would be expensive.

In all we chose 16 countries:

1. Canada
2. America
3. Costa Rica
4. Panama
5. Guatemala
6. Argentina
7. Peru
8. New Zealand
9. Australia
10. Bali
11. Singapore
12. Thailand
13. Vietnam
14. Cambodia
15. India
16. Nepal

Most of my family are very traditional, Nannie & Grandad owned their own home, as did my Mum & Aunt. My Uncle on the other hand lived on a bus in Sudbury woods. He was a dreadlocked nomad, and since the year 2000 no-one has seen him. He used to come and go sporadically but one time he didn't come back. I could understand why my family were hesitant to support me giving up the only stable home I had ever had for myself. Although I wanted to give up rent, council tax, and an address for a year I would keep in touch with them and never intentionally go missing which evidence suggests is the case with Uncle Michael.

Once I told my Mum the news that the flat would be going I started to look at what I could sell. My mantra at the time was: 'earn money – get on a plane'. My goal was to save as much as possible over the year leading up to our departure and max out some credit cards while travelling. I estimated I would spend about £25,000 when we were away, a similar amount to what I would earn in a year working for the Lincolnshire Echo. I figured it would take me a few years of laying low, after the trip, to pay it all back.

I had been in my sales job for 9 years, I sold advertising, managed a monthly magazine and was a digital media specialist. I often got a good bonus but the stress of working in an increasingly toxic atmosphere of redundancies and pressure pushed me to take the plunge into self-employment. I had already dipped my toe in the water by writing blogs and managing a clients Twitter account for £100 a month. Once I put my mind to it I had 4 clients and an income of £1300 a month. The transition from employed to self employed was not as terrifying as I had preempted it to be for the decade I had procrastinated. For extra cash I put my Reiki and massage qualifications to use.

Our flights were cheaper than we anticipated, which we booked with STA travel (Start the Adventure) at their Nottingham branch. I used this company to travel to Thailand and India on their YOLO trips, (you only live once). The great thing about this company was that their 'Round the World' trips started from £1000. Seventeen flights, travel insurance and a bus trip around New Zealand, which happened to be half price on the day we were in the shop, came to £3,500 each. Within this price too was a 'Multi-Flex' product for £100 each which would allow us to change the dates of our flights and only pay the difference in tax. We used biro on a throwaway map in the shop to plan our route. We kept this map the whole year we were away as a memento of our dream coming to life.

SELLING STUFF

I thought I would keep my guitar and my solid-oak writers' desk but then decided I would test the universe, would it deliver me something better once I had let these things go? My gorgeous green leather topped desk went to Ebay's highest bidder. I later realised the symbolism that I could now work from anywhere. I have since worked from a Las Vegas RV park Laundry room and carried my 'office' every place we visited around the world. I even took my laptop caving in Costa Rica as I didn't trust leaving it in our rainforest cabin. I couldn't have climbed down a 50ft ladder into a beautiful prehistoric cave while I was still chained to a desk!

My guitar was the hardest thing to let go, it was my first and only. An 'Epiphone Dove' which I had brought with my first-year student loan in 2004. 'Another guitar would come to me if it was right', I reasoned, after the money had been added to my travelling fund. Once I had sold almost everything I owned and moved into Anna's attic I started selling her stuff too! We agreed to go 50/50 on the profits, she had recently broken up with Scott and memories of their relationship littered the house. Emotionally she couldn't face sorting through the drawers, the gifts and his old possessions. Also she couldn't stand to use the selling sites and have strangers come to the door. I took control and we filled a skip, and I dealt with the online buyers earning hundreds between us. Enough to cover my rent to her. By the time we left I had £5k in the bank and over £12k a year projected earnings from 'Just B Social' , my new 'creative nomad' company. I had never had a credit card before but I was able to get £15,000 in available credit from various banks. I had access to £32,000, well over my projected £25k I thought I needed. We had no idea how much travelling the world was going to cost at this point but I had heard from friends who had done it that they had underestimated the costs. The same friends had cut their trip short after surviving on one 'Pot Noodle' a day in Asia! Luke had been fighting for 10 years for a criminal injury payout, from the vicious attack in 2006. His final court date was pending and he had already refused £30,000 as his injuries changed his whole life. Whatever the next offer of compensation was, it would be his funding for the trip.

THE LEAVING PARTY

After a year as Luke's girlfriend I had gained enough experience seeing him inebriated to know that our leaving party would be eventful. I was anxious about his behavior, especially as my Mum, Stepdad, Auntie and many lifelong friends would be there. His behaviour was out of anyone's control and by 2:30 in the afternoon he was being rude to people. I had a fab day of singing on stage, clearing the rest of our stuff via a table top tombola and spending quality time with my family and best friends. I sang with my old band mate Iain and then aca-pella and invited the guests to come and do the same. Once it started raining, we sought shelter in a large bathroom which had a golden chair in one corner. I sat on the chair with all my girlfriends around me. I was happy and I hoped that drink and party drugs weren't going to be a part of our new life together on the road, and that once we left Newark things would get easier.

We had both been really excited about the party, I wore my Sari while Luke wore his kilt! A lovely family of Indian women helped me tie my Sari, Luke had been at school with one of the girls and had not hesitated in knocking on the door and asking them to help me with my complicated outfit. I wouldn't have been able to wear that Sari if Luke hadn't put himself out and asked for help. Luke and I had been for romantic dinners a few times at the pub where our leaving party was, each time I felt like a princess. The majority of the time Luke behaves like a true gent but when he's had too much to drink, or smoked weed he's an absolute nightmare: cue Manic Mick.

Unfortunately our leaving party turned out to be one of those times he wanted a 'blow out' this remains a good reason why we'll never have a traditional wedding day. (Too much risk of the same thing happening again). Mental illness and drugs/alcohol collide with disastrous results. After the party no-one heard from Luke until 4pm the next day. We had given up Luke's flat by this point and were living at his Nans. We were due to have a farewell lunch and my parents were taking Bruiser to live with them for the time we would be away. He didn't show up at the house in the morning, no-one knew where he was so after lunch the dog had been taken and Luke didn't get to say goodbye.

My mum asked his Nan if this is something Luke does often. Dawny was horrified, she said he'd not done anything like this in the whole time that she had known him. Josh asked me 'Where's Uncle D?', I had no idea. My mum asked me what I would say to him. I said probably nothing. I felt happy and calm so that I could enjoy the company I did have. I thought that he would turn up eventually as I waited for him to wake up and come home.

A beautiful disaster – Blog 31st July 2017

"I'm going travelling with someone who doesn't think his hayfever will be a problem out of the UK. I'm going travelling tomorrow with someone who has just sold his car but gave the buyer the key to his Nans car as well as the Ford.

After going missing from our leaving party he returned minus his debit card for a brand-new account in which his first month's travel fund resides. I had to drive Dawny's car 20 miles down the A46 to pick up an empty man-bag in a fruitless attempt to collect

Luke's belongings.

He missed supporting me through a sad conga line of goodbyes yesterday. I was fine though. We had a laugh over lunch all of us – despite the lingering fear that if it got any later we'd be calling the missing person's helpline. Luke is not my responsibility, he is responsible for himself but he does a shitty job sometimes. I love him and respect that as soon as he was reunited with his phone he called my parents and apologised to them, explaining that heavy drinking was not going to play a part in our year away.

Understandably my Mum is worried we would both be locked up before the end of the first week. I had some difficult questions put to me over the weekend, do I understand what I'm taking on? Am I mentally prepared? For reasons I'm yet to explore: all of my old boyfriends have had an array of major mental health and person-ality issues combined with varying degrees of substance abuse.

Generally Luke's a beautiful inspiration. Sometimes he's a beau-tiful disaster. He's giving me a foot massage right now asking re-peatedly if I'm his favourite. I have to smile at his ability to not be bogged down by his own ineptitude and how he finds the energy to keep swinging the wrecking ball into various points of THE DAY BEFORE WE TRAVEL.

Thank you to everyone who came to the leaving do. It was brilliant! Becca xx"

HEATHROW TO CALGARY, CANADA

On the train as we left Newark for London Luke caught me Googling; 'How to take care of someone'. So many people had told us to take care of each other. I just wanted to make sure I had the best information. Google said: 'Ask the other person if they are ok, do little things for them.' I can manage that I thought.

I was anxious on the train I thought about terrorist attacks. Statistically I'm sure our visit to Istanbul a few months before was more risky but I didn't watch Istanbul news. I watched the BBC coverage of 7/7 and the killings on London bridge. I had tried twice the night before to check us in with Air Canada and then 4 times at various machines amongst the swarms of travellers and their 1000 bags of un-checked baggage. I realised the name on my ticket didn't match the one on my passport. Assuming that my missing middle name was the root of the problem, I panicked and I suggested: "Let's go to Paris instead". I thought they wouldn't let me board our plane and we would have to go back to Newark, our world trip faltering at the very first step. As we were waiting to check in Luke remained calm while we called the travel agent who confirmed that changing the name on all of our tickets would mean re-booking the whole trip which would 'incur penalties.' I was frantic. In the end we realised we couldn't do an online check in because we had a connecting flight, the issue wasn't with my name, and all the panic and stress was unnecessary. We wanted to travel light but our overstuffed backpacks were not light! Luke had already binned his 'Crocodile Dundee' hat to keep accessories to a minimum.

I watched two French subtitled films on the way to French speaking Calgary. The sick bags or 'Sac Malaise' in the bathroom reminded me that at the height of my high-school rebellion, my friends and I would learn phrases that weren't on the curriculum and loudly yell them at each other around school. I loved everything about school. Whereas Luke used to leave his school during the day and visit another and pretend to be a student there. They had the exact same uniform apart from the tie. (He would borrow a tie!) He attended Art, Geography and English before he was asked into the Headmasters office to explain himself. At his own school he would do P.E with his class and then pretend to be in the year below to repeat the lesson. His creation of 'Double P.E' led the way to his non-stop focus on personal training and love of sport. He would "go skiving" at a friend's house to avoid lessons or full days at school. It's a good job opposites attract!

LUKE'S PERSONALITIES

After his head injury Luke was diagnosed with a personality deficit which is also known as a split personality disorder. These are the different personalities I have met or heard of since meeting him.

1. Tommy Concrete

Tommy makes an appearance some mornings, he's all muscle, communicating only with his biceps, puffed up shoulders and arms. He'll fill the door, blocking my way to have my morning wee, he just needs a 'Morning Tommy' and he'll soon be gone again. The first few times I met him I tried to just shove him out of the way, but he is a concrete boulder, so I quickly realised there was no chance.

2. Luke

I met on our first date and he is the one who wooed me for the months after and most days since. He looks after me and makes me a hot drink every morning followed by breakfast in bed. He loves me and I love him. I looked into his eyes on our first date and I saw that he knew how to take responsibility for his mental health and that he didn't need saving. He had saved himself. Luke cuddles me when I'm upset, reassures me when I'm doubting myself, keeps me on track to achieve my dreams. He also goes overboard with planning my birthday and Christmas presents and spoils me often. Luke is the only person I know of in the world who spends his first waking moments looking on

Facebook to see who's birthday it is so he can write a heartfelt birthday message to them.

3. Sensible Sam
I met Sam once on the high mountain roads in Yosemite national park, he negotiated a hair pin bend incredibly deftly and I liked him immensely.

4. Manic Mick
A fucking nightmare from start to finish. Just stay out of his way. Mick comes out when Luke has smoked weed. Manic, talking a thousand words a minute, opinionated with no actual opinion other than to talk over you. Orders people around. Belligerent. Extremely argumentative and delusional. Terrifyingly, Mick can also take over Luke and all other personalities when Luke has a breakdown. Everyone who cares about him wants him to get help, to return back to Luke but Mick is always right and knows best so we just have to ride it out until Luke returns.

5. Depressive Dan.
Sadly Dan mopes in when Mick has exhausted Luke's body by keeping him awake for the mania days/weeks. Dan over thinks, can't find the motivation or self belief to do anything but question the bad decisions and wallow.

6. Dyno.
Fun-time adventure Luke with a little mania. Loves team sports and training people, being the life and soul of the party without upsetting anyone. An enthusiastic and motivational friend. Dyno is short for Dynomite as that was his Football nickname from his younger days.

7. Coco Wallace.
A cross between Coco the clown and William Wallace. Basically the worst it can and has ever got for Luke. Luke was Coco Wallace when he was sectioned. Coco Wallace smokes weed while in a secure mental unit, tells people how to do their job using

Luke's knowledge of working for the NHS, complains and causes so much upset that he is moved to another secure unit. I never want to meet him. I imagine him a step too far past Manic Mick. Dyno will dress up like Coco Wallace at festivals, with his face painted blue, wearing a kilt. I was surprised when he said he liked the name Wallace for a son if we had one. Wouldn't he prefer to forget that extremely volatile personality that got him sectioned? No, he said, "I wanted to change my name from Luke to Wallace when Luke was dead to me. I was too ashamed to be Luke, Wallace saved me."

8   Dangerous Bryan / Dangerous Bri.
Dangerous Bri was mentioned in passing in a conversation between Luke and his friend 2 days after we booked our flights around the world. Dangerous Bri I imagine is the person who broke out of the secure unit to go to Leeds Festival.

9.   Morris/ Moaning Morris.
 God help me, Morris loves a moan. I'm still learning how to deal with him. Morris wears me out! He will moan about everything. I've tried telling myself it's a symptom of depression, but the moaning strips away my empathy within seconds. Luke has advised me to say 'Alright Morris' when he's moaning to bring humour to the situation.

I should mention that I now have a few personalities courtesy of Luke highlighting them.

1. Becca - the passionate, sparkly eyed girl with a posh voice he fell in love with on our first date.

2. PMT Polly - Pre-mentrual tension personified, no energy, ratty, tense, tearful, hungry, tired, bloated, Becca is locked deep inside Polly unable to speak up.

3. Make out Maureen - when I'm 'making out' that things are worse than they are. Morris's sidekick.

4. Maureen the witch-faced arsehole. A pumped up version of Maureen when I've really upset Luke.

5. Dangerous Brenda, the sidekick he creates for me when Dangerous Brian is devising a plan.

Sadly Luke's extreme mental health problems led him down the path of attempted suicide. Travel makes him feel alive, it makes him well. I couldn't wait for us to start living the life we were planning.

FEAR OF DEATH

The first time I was scared of dying on our trip was driving on the high roads in British Columbia (BC). We took some time to realize that; British Columbia was a 'province' of Canada, and the whole of Canada isn't just called Canada. On a road trip toward the Rocky Mountains with absolutely no clue where we were, in our borrowed car, on the wrong side of the road, it was pitch black and hammering down with rain. We were on mountain roads with a sheer drop on at least one side and both of us were really tired. It was a recipe for disaster. You know when you tell someone to take care when they go off on a trip? It is times like those that your words will echo in their head. Luke had gone to sleep in the passenger side while I was driving with limited visibility. The weather was really bad and we were miles away from anything that resembled civilisation.

Our only option that night was to sleep in the car. We pulled off the road but I was afraid that people would come and move us on. We felt pretty exposed and it was difficult to get to sleep, however with the aid of the heated seats we managed it! The scary experience was overshadowed by views of the mountains the next morning which were breathtaking. We soon forgot about the journey and the restless night – we had arrived in the Canadian Rockies!

How did we get this far?

Being eternally free-spirited and blindly hopeful that 'things would work out' we had only pre-booked two nights accommodation for our 365 days away. This was a hostel for the 1st & 2nd night of our trip in central Vancouver.

Before this trip together I had never travelled away from home without all the accommodation booked in advance. Luke had travelled Thailand negotiating on hostel prices as he went, so I trusted in his experience. Although the only thing I really learned from him was "you can't haggle with a ladyboy". The Vancouver hostel turned out to be a nightclub with basic rooms above it, there were metal bunk beds, a wooden floor, loads of metal lockers and a door with a dodgy lock. We had to walk all the way round the other side of the building to use the loo. That's what you get for less than $30 a night I guessed. Quickly realising that hostels full of students over a booming club, that doesn't close until 3am on a 'quiet night', wasn't for us, we re-searched other options. We had heard of Airbnb, where you stay in a spare room in someone's house but I was dubious of using them in England as I had read about hosts setting up cameras in the bedroom. We came back to our hostel on the second night, after a day of exploring the busy streets of Vancouver, to see hundreds of young Canadians partying and filling the 'sidewalk' around the bar. We were a bit old for this and would have to take the risk of the night cameras in the bedroom instead!

Vancouver was a brilliant city with a unique steam clock and the nicest and most helpful residents you could imagine. People volunteered to help us at every junction as we couldn't read a map, even a map of a city that's a convenient grid design. Sadly in Vancouver there were a lot of heroin users everywhere though they seemed friendly. One street was full of tents like terraced houses, we both felt uneasy about walking past the homeless people who were selling meagre possessions on dirty sheets. This was not the experience we anticipated but we real-ised there is light and dark to every place.

To get away from the city, we walked over the Capilano sus-pension bridge which felt wobbly underfoot, high above the

Capilano River and forest canopies. The smell of the trees was intoxicating. Back on lower ground I had tree sap drip on me, it smelt incredible, like the best cedarwood oil you can imagine, natural, fresh and deep. We had ideas about launching it as an alcohol free scent for eco warriors – simply called 'SAP'. We were happier with trees than with skyscrapers. I was feeling really excited about the year ahead, we had placed ourselves right outside our comfort zones. Our first week in Vancouver we found our feet as travellers. We got on our first 'Greyhound Bus' from Vancouver to Whistler, then on to our first Airbnb, in Pemberton, a small town a few miles away from the ski villiage Whistler.

MEET POLLY

PMT Polly arrived in an otherwise perfectly quaint Whistler for the first time since England. Her attitude was the worst it had ever been. I had a rather painful procedure to remove dangerous cervical cells the month before our trip so my uterus was in no mood for a period in the blazing Canadian heat. Polly insisted she only wanted to lay down which she did on the nearest patch of grass. There was a man selling tours and with it being out of season was promising lifts to the top of various mountains. Luke was negotiating with him to get more value for money than he was already offering. While the two of them negociated a trip Polly had no intention of taking, Polly lost her shit and declared Whistler a 'fucking nightmare'. We searched around for somewhere to stay but the hotels were $300 a night. As we weren't staying in a nearby hotel the salesman withdrew his offer of a cheap tour and Polly got her way. We were leaving Whistler, which I'm sure on any other time of the month would have got top marks on Tripadvisor.

Our first ever host, 'Paul Wilson', (originally from Yorkshire) and his native Canadian wife, Korey, set the bar so high for our Airbnb, we were converts after our first stay. Paul thankfully fetched us from the bus stop near his home, despite it being almost midnight once we arrived, we got a pitch black tour of the town regardless.

We longed to visit the Canadian Rocky Mountains. The snow capped peaks, glacial lakes, day hikes and the risk of bears called to our sense of adventure. We had done some hiking but Lincoln only has one hill ('Steep Hill'), which leads to the Cathedral. We were excited to conquer some real mountains! After a few days of struggling to find a campervan for hire we were getting nowhere, as it was high season. We kept having to extend our stay with Paul & Korey because we couldn't find a way to the mountains. There had been some forest fires affecting the bus and train routes and all the travel advice said you really need to be in your own vehicle to experience the Rockies.

For a small fee Paul drove us out to Joffre Lakes, where we had a great day visiting waterfalls and three glacial lakes. Luke had a swim after falling off a tree into freezing cold water! It was a perfect day, aside from being bitten by horse flies anytime either of us stood still. Picking us up after our day of hiking, Paul said even though he had lived in this area for years he had never been to Joffre lakes. He empathised with our plight of not being able to find transport to the Rockies and offered to loan us his father's old car which had been sitting in the garage for a few months since his passing. He was keen to help us but mindful that we had only just met so he asked us to provide a couple of character references from home to prove that we were who we claimed to be! An email from a friend back home quelled his worries and we were finally getting somewhere. Paul charged us $600 for the car rental and gave us everything we needed for 10 days in the Rockies. The Lexus car had temperature-controlled leather seats and a good supply of Mentos which we thanked 'Grandpa Wilson' for each time we had one. Paul from Pemberton's kindness assured us that we had made the right decision in being free-spirited around our accommodation plans.

We argued a lot in Pemberton, a couple of days before we set off for the road trip, we had an argument that ended with me sprinting off in a different direction at a pace that surprised the both of us. Luke couldn't find me, after a bit of time waiting for him to track me down I decided to drink some wine at the bar. After hours and hours Luke appeared online, by which time I had befriended an old man. Luke came down and we all enjoyed dinner together. The man had blown a tire so was stuck in town, we offered him a drink and he did the same for us, it turned out that this old man's whiskey was about $25 a serving which we had a good laugh about, after we got over the shock. Once Luke couldn't find me, he'd gone on a solo trek to find a waterfall in bear territory, not the wisest move. Meeting other people turned out to be helpful in taking the pressure off each other.

Before we said our goodbyes to Paul & Korey I gave Korey a Reiki treatment in return for an interview. I loved hearing about her native Candian roots and learning about the new land we'd arrived at on a deeper level.

KOREY'S STORY

"Paul & I were sacked from our jobs when they found out we were together. We were both working as Social Workers for the First Nation families in BC. I'm a First Nation, my Grandpa was a chief.

I was featured in a film called 'no-surrender' about the history of where I'm from. I travelled with my Dad throughout North America fighting for the environment. The First Nations and indigenous people gather together every 2 years to get support and address our environmental issues. Our issue was stopping Kemano 2, a man-made dam. They wanted to take the Geslato River and use all that water, if they did we would be without a lake, it was a disaster.

Dad was a counsellor and we spoke to whoever was listening. I did a lot of protests in the States and Canada. I stand up for native people, I wanted to go to North Dakota to protest but Paul wouldn't let me.

You have to give people hope that their traditions aren't dying. I grew up watching my great grandma just be. She was a traditional medicine woman, gathering herbs and medicine from the land. My mum was one of the people who were displaced by the flood from a prior man-made dam which devastated the lives of our people.

For first nation people being at one with the earth is our spirituality, for me personally it's a sacred thing, I don't tell my son because he would follow my sacred thing, I want him to have his own, for me it's doing a lot of meditation, saying a lot of prayers in the morning to God and the creator. Even if you see someone stranded by the side of the road, I say a quick prayer & hope that they do well on their journey.

I've not had Reiki before but there is a therapist who treats our community. We have a lot of abuse amongst First Nation people & they don't like to be touched, they don't like to be massaged, it brings back a lot of horrible memories.

Because of the abuse in the residential schools, a lot of people only know bad touch, whether that was physical or sexual. It's really sad. I've seen one person who didn't want to be touched so the therapist just had them lay on the massage table and with the essential oils the music they were able to relax without being touched. During my Reiki session I was reminded of a cartoon of a duck, the duck is perfectly serene above the water & it's not until you look under the surface that you realise the legs are going like crazy."

THE ROCKIES

The morning we left for the Rockies, we found ourselves pulling into our first 'Rodeo'. The food, locals and the fearless cowboys trying to stay on bucking bulls was a culture shock for us. We stayed for a few hours, laughing about how, because the cook at the barbeque took her time cutting the salad to go with my hot-dog. I asked for 'Tomaayta' in an american accent instead of 'Tomato' in my usual Queen's English, in case she had misunderstood my initial request. The hotdog was so good it disappeared by the time I turned around to admire some passing snakeskin boots. A convoy of cars came into the rodeo, all beeping and 'hollering'. They were celebrating a wedding and we were enjoying ourselves as much as the convoy.

That night, we were heading to a campground which we had put into Grandpa Wilson's sat nav. We actually ended up at a native Indian Reserve called 'Mooch'. According to the Garmin there wasn't a campground for another 49 miles. As we turned the car around our saviour came out of nowhere: 'Blue Lake Camping Ground'. We circled up the side of a mountain, via a dirt track, it was 8pm by this point and we were ready for a rest. It was either this campground or another hour drive using our dodgy GPS.

As we queued at the check-in-hut, hoping they had space for our tent, a beautiful Hummingbird came to drink at a water dish above our heads, I relaxed, I knew we would be ok here. Luke thought it was a good sign that he swam at 'Blue Lake' in Newark as a kid. After speaking with my family back home, it transpired that my Auntie Karen and Nannie had been here years previously on their visit to my Grandad's brother's place, it was strange because they hadn't been camping!

I felt that Nannie was guiding us here. We had thought we were following directions to 'Cache Creek' but when we later checked we were 40 miles away from there. Luke got talking to the owner and once we had set our tent up he drove round to us to drop off a couple of cold beers! We made a picnic and sat down to watch 'Hook' the Disney film that was just starting at their open air cinema. Thank god we didn't go to Cache Creek, this place was literally perfect, cold beer, warm starry night, picnic and a Disney film. We were in bliss. I made little cheese and salad Ryvitas, really loving that we were looking after each other and bonding over the small things like finding somewhere to sleep, eating and watching a film. Luke especially was in his element, his mental health problems took a back seat when we had the focus of setting up a tent and discovering a new part of the world.

The next day we hiked up a trail in Fraser Valley, where we met two friendly and helpful older men with a dog. They advised on what route we should take for the rest of our 'Rocky Road Trip', what places to eat at and certain shortcuts to take to avoid paying to see local 'attractions'. We reached the summit of Blue Mountain together and the view was like Jurassic Park. We saw giant Turkey vultures flying in the distance over a massive green canyon. Canada is gigantic on an unbelievable scale. There are mountains and waterfalls at every corner. Randy (one of the men) said that even Americans make the mistake of thinking Canada can be seen in a short road trip but it would take you 5 days to see British Columbia; that's just one province of ten. (We were beginning to get an idea!)

Later the owner of the campground, Jim, played bagpipes for us, Luke had told him he was half Scottish and it turned out Jim's family was from Scotland generations ago. I love bagpipes and have always said I want them at my imaginary wedding. I've had no Scottish connection but now I do in Luke. Because Luke chatted to Jim when we arrived we got special treatment and a lovely send off. I can be embarrassed about striking up conversations with strangers but it turned out that talking to people is a massive benefit to travelling the world.

We went to visit Hell's Gate, with the assumption that Randy and his friend had given us decent advice. They said it's where the salmon swim up the river and the gap they have to get through is just a foot wide. When we arrived it was nothing of the sort. It was a giant canyon we had to climb down with the knowledge that we would have to climb all the way out of 'Hell' again. At the bottom we found a massive river where fish and the Titanic would have had plenty of room to get through plus a really boring fish museum. We had a nice lunch of an interesting Chicken Caesar Salad that was actually Salmon, then got on our way once again.

—

Blog: Rocky Mountain Roadtrip (Written by Luke.)

Following a short, opposite side of the road driving lesson from Paul we leave Pemberton heading for the Rocky Mountains lunchtime, Saturday 12th August 2017. It's a gorgeous 34 degrees outside. Paul kindly lent us his camping set up - a double burner stove, 2 man tent, blow up double ground mat, gas burner light, pots n pans, cool box and luxury picnic hamper looks brand spanking! Not to mention the top of the range Lexus 330, 2.8 litre auto flying machine.

We goes to fill the motor up, Paul has asked us to put premium in $1.38, the standard is $1.14, and we're gonna be filling a few times, so me as the budget planner (tight arse) after asking 3 locals who say standard will be fine says could we maybe use standard? Becca (miss honesty) wants to fill with premium as it says on petrol cap "premium only" what would you do?

The highlights from our 10 day Rocky Mountain road trip by Luke...

A round up of viewpoints, national parks, and activities we did together... Places we stayed in, visited, survived and thrived including Yoho Glacier, Banff and Jasper national parks. Lakes we swam in and or drank from including Lake Lousie, Lakes Moraine, Athabasca, Superior, Kootenay and the 39 degree radium hot springs. Icefields parkway, one of the most scenic drives in the world... the Banff Gondola ride and the mountains we hiked including Tunnel 1692m to its summit and Sulphur mountain which is 2,451m.

We felt Mountains in England were quite intimidating to hike but Sulphur mountain we climbed dwarfs Ben Nevis and it gave us a massive confidence boost to try new things. This has been happening every day which is the challenge and joy of travelling. Naturewise we witnessed a humpback whale breach (jump out of the water), saw bear, caribou, deer, numerous birds, a grass snake, giant spiders and ants. We fed chipmunks and a bird. We practiced yoga together daily, attended a class in Banff and were invited back to teach. We laughed, we danced, we sang, we argued but most of all we lived the dream. We shared 1900 miles in 10 days and camped out across Canada and the Rockies for 9 nights....Boom, what a first month! 2 shite things about the Rocky Mountains... terrible wifi and the thinnest toilet paper the world!

For some reason dangerous Brian & Brenda (us) decided to skip Glacier campground (which I had booked us into) to head for Golden a town just before the Rockies...we still get charged $25 for not showing. Golden is more like brass.. brass monkeys as the *camping was freezing. In the morning we set off on a 6km hike to the rotary loop recommended by camp staff, visibility was poor due to forest fires, waste of a walk really. So we did another 4km hike on mount revelstoke to the waterfall there, which was beautiful. On the way back to the campsite we stopped at a log cabin bar and had a few cocktails. It was so cold and we suddenly realised the sleeping bags had not been packed but very much needed! We toss and turn snuggled like sardines all night freezing cold with one thin cover.*

We survive the night, thriving in general. Head chef Brenda is keeping us eating fairly healthy and on budget with breakfast omelettes, cereal, tuna salads, Ryvita snacks and noodles. All cooked on the camping stove we borrowed. Camp-supervisor Bri is keeping the campsite ticking over!

—

Once our mountain road trip was finished we returned the car to Pemberton and looked into moving on to Toronto. We planned to get the bus but a quick Google search returned no routes, further actual research revealed that Toronto was almost 3000 miles away, our only option without flying would be a 4 day train trip. I fretted while looking at the screen, we were crossing the whole of Canada only to come back this way again in a few weeks to San Francisco which was just a 2 hour flight away. It would have been logical for our first flight from the UK to go to Toronto but on the 1st August my family didn't have room for us as my cousin was visiting them. It would have made sense financially and logistically to delay the trip until my family had room. Unfortunately we aren't financially or logistically minded, we're romantics and we wanted our trip to start on the anniversary of our first date. The cheapest flights I could find from Vancouver to Toronto were $782 dollars, I made a mistake by assuming I was buying in Candian dollars rather than USD. This cost me a further £150 and they weren't even direct flights! I really hoped we had made the right decision to forgo sensible route planning.

BLOG - AT THE COTTAGE: BECCA

31st August 2017

I'm so tired from the camping so I stay inside my Great Aunt and Uncle's swish Condo while Luke cycles a 31 miles round trip to every single possible site in the gigantic city of Toronto. He arrives back almost completely asleep but just in time for a lovely roast dinner and family gathering.

The next morning we set off for the cottage via the 'Canadian Superstore' where we spend $100 on surplus snacks in-case the cottage supply dries up. In fact when we arrive there are already 4 fridges & freezers full to the brim! At the Cottage there is no WIFI. Will we both slip into a depressive coma due to lack of activity & mental stimulation? Will we succumb to cabin fever or be a burden for octogenarian's Chris & John who prefer the slower pace of life?

The cottage is a place to grow a bigger pot-belly, a place to sleep until 10:30, have breakfast, then go for a nap. Aunt Chris has a feast on the table for 6pm every evening, complete with a ready poured glass of wine & accompanying salad. We enjoy broccoli & bacon salad, maple syrup pancakes, a third helping of cauliflower-cheese pasta. Luke's subtle hints that I should be doing more 'planks' and cardio continue to go ignored. We hiked 9 miles yesterday. A walk we had with cousin Debbie topped those even in the Rockies. We jumped through swamps, crossed rivers & waterfalls and climbed stacks of boulders higher than a house.

Giant, jet-black squirrels steal nuts from the feeders, while the almost tame Chipmunks hoover up seeds from the floor. Blue-Jays visit while the tree-creepers silently slide down trunks. We love it here. We inhabit a second cottage at the end of the garden 'the bunkie' featuring gingham curtains and 35-year-old National Geographic magazines. We talk about spending the year here or possibly our lives. We can't believe our luck and we profess our love for each other and cuddle. There's a 95% reduction in the amount we argue, we get lost on a canoe and remain as peaceful as the water.

We needed this break, after hiking the Rockies, sleeping outside or in the car while temperatures reached as low as 1' we owed it to our bodies to recoup. After 5 days of sleeping 9 – 10 hours a night we are not ready to leave just yet. We will make the most of tomorrow by swimming and fishing in the lake via paddleboat. We are heading to San Francisco on Monday. Our travelling will restart but I doubt we will find a retreat as relaxing as this elsewhere in the world... The search starts now.

SAN-FRANCISCO

4th September 2017

We are told by our host that San Francisco's 'Cable Cars' are not to be missed. So we headed to the train station for a ride into the city. Luke nips to the cash machine while I walk ahead to look into buying our tickets. I wait for a bit and then a bit longer. Luke has been about half an hour before he arrives with a story to tell. He had forgotten his pin, had input the wrong pin three times and had his card swallowed by the machine. He then had a debate with two members of staff about getting the card back. Apparently they had a policy of not giving back swallowed cards. Luke pleaded with them and said it was his only means of financing his trip so eventually they handed it back. What an unnecessary drama!

We get to the City Centre and the 'cable cars' are nowhere to be seen, we hop on a tram and it's a fun experience to hang off the side and view the city with the wind in our hair. We hop off and enjoy a chowder for lunch which is a creamy fish soup served inside a bread roll. We decide to invest in a two day pass on a bus tour of the city and discover that the 1967 Summer of love was born here when thousands of hippies converged in the neighborhood of Haight-Ashbury. I bought a green tie-dye dress and we had a couple of beers while window shopping for guitars.

The tour guide told us that Golden Gate Bridge's orange/red colour was originally meant to serve only as the primer. Once we got back to our host's place and explained we couldn't find the 'cable-cars' she was perplexed. It turned out that we were both talking a different language. In America they call trams cable cars. In the UK I understood these to be something you catch to the top of a mountain if you wanted to ski down it. All morning in the city we were looking up in search of ski-lifts from the tram. Apparently they call ski-lifts Gonderlers. The confusion goes on and I wondered what they call the boats you can ride in Venice!

The next day the bus tour is becoming a little repetitive and we can recite the history of the place before it's announced. We have a favourite tour guide and one or two we don't really rate. Some of the facts are questionable as there are inconsistencies between what one guide says and what the other claims - maybe we should have just got a one day tour! We jump off at Fisherman's Wharf for a second lunch of chowder and we discover a crowd of people looking out at the water. We see what must be 100 sea lions. We learn the colony has been living by pier 39 since an earthquake in 1989. It was incredible to be so close to nature at a touristy dining spot, we loved the unexpected meeting.

–

It felt unnatural to want – so badly to get *into* Alcatraz the infamous prison. I was looking forward to it because the film with Clint Eastwood was brilliant. As we stood on the dock I thought about how I longed to feel free while I was working 9-5 but while travelling I'd become anxious to find a Wi-Fi signal to do work. I was feeling I created my own trap by bringing a business with me on the road but I needed to earn money to keep supporting myself.

"You cannot take from a man the thought that he wants his freedom." – Alcatraz tour sign.

There were lots of flies and bird-crap on Alcatraz, a big part of me wished we had stayed at the Airbnb, with Polly beginning to surface. Luke had treated us to a nice place with a pool and hot tub but as this was our last night in San Francisco we had 'had' to double book ourselves and go on this tour. We were at the mercy of Manic Mick wanting to do all the things and needing to be in two places at once. Despite wishing Luke had just gone to Alcatraz without me I enjoyed an art exhibition by inmates at other prisons, some of whom were still serving their time. Art and poetry was an outlet for them to feel free despite being confined to their cell.

We enjoyed our few days in San Francisco, as soon as we arrived, our host, a Chinese realtor, mentioned that Las Vegas was a 4-hour drive away, without a word to each other a road trip was decided. We only had 9 days until our flight out of LA to Guatemala so we had to get a move on and find an RV for driving from San Francisco.

Becca Blog: If you're going to San-Francisco, be sure to be aware of EL Monte RV rental.

13th September 2017

"I give up, that's it. This was a bad idea. We know nothing about RV's. I'm not even sure what RV stands for. Yet we're driving a 25ft, 2 bed model down a 5-lane freeway in the dark, with no clue where the next campground is.

We negotiated a late check out at 2pm today and 20 minutes later we were at the RV rental place. When I say 'RV rental place' I mean; 'the centre of excellence at maximising profits from RV rentals'. The kid that 'served' us, incredibly, knew nothing of any use relating to RV's but when it came to being inflexible about prices; he really excelled.

> *• $819 deposit (he was very vague about what this*

covered as he said the booking had come through an agent, aka we'd booked online.)

- $125 for a kitchen-kit (pots, pans, kettle, salad bowl, jug, 1 cup, 1 glass, some cutlery. In hind-sight we could have bought this ourselves and then given them to a homeless person after the trip. Homeless people are not hard to find, our taxi driver from the train station was homeless, well, he lived in the car which smelt absolutely rank. On the plus-side he looked exactly like Morgan Freeman and shared with us his shocking and tragic life-story up to the point that we'd gotten into the car.

- $185 prep fee (We were meant to pick up at 10am, which we extended to 1pm (hot tub time) and then didn't manage to get there until 2:20pm. The RV was nowhere to be seen & we discovered by about 4pm that it was having its battery changed! We may have a case for claiming back the 'prep' fee seeing as it was 'prepped' during our rental time.

- $87 for estimated 300 extra miles over the 500 we initially paid for – god forbid we go over our allocated mileage. I believe that it's $32 dollars per 100 miles over 800. We make a plan to push it back to LA.

- $50 "Convenience Kit" this is in air quote marks as it's pretty "inconvenient" to have a kit for one person. It leaves the other person waiting hungrily for the cereal bowl and spoon while 'the convenienced one' gets use of the kit which strictly caters for one person. The salesman really earnt his stripes here by refusing to offer a second convenience kit for any less than $50. I said we would buy a blanket if need be as he was very unclear whether the package we paid for included enough warmth for two *people. (turns out it did include two blankets and it's about 100 degrees so we are fine!)*

- *$40 generator fee – from what I can work-out the generator powers the only two plug sockets in the RV which are inexplicably right next to the toilet. Maybe they have a fee for septic tank iphone retrieval – anywhere between $75 – $300.*

- *$350 drop fee, a fee to drop off the bloody bankrupting giant van-box! Because we are dropping in LA and we picked up in San Fran we have to sell a kidney. We discovered all of these add-ons only after they had taken to initial deposit so we had to either carry on with it or lose £600.*

So, it turns out that it's always darkest before dawn. I literally gave up on life whilst driving through a static-caravan-village Luke had claimed was an RV park; the residents had no idea where we should park the RV. We got back onto the Freeway and had a shouting match over my phone running out of battery, it was 9pm, we were hungry and tired.

Our saviour came in the form of a small place called 'Jenny Elk RV park'. We tracked Jenny down by driving around the site three times before asking what turned out to be the most helpful and knowledgeable couple; Marty & Larry. They helped us plug our van in or: 'hook up' as it seemed it was called.

We made the bed which surprisingly accommodated the two of us. I re-opened the red wine I bought with us from the night before and all is well with the world. I loved the RV. I apologised to Luke for saying the RV idea was stupid. If we hadn't gone for it we wouldn't have had a chance to overcome a fear of driving a-giant-house around foreign lands. We're driving to Vegas via Yosemite national park to win back the thousands of dollars El Monte RV Rental managed to charge us in unavoidable add-ons."

DEATH VALLEY

11th September 2017

"I see a couple of flashes in the distance, I think I'm imagining it, as its daylight, there are no clouds and its boiling hot, not like storms I remember from the rain soaked dark storms of my childhood. We're driving the RV through Death Valley, we've come from Yosemite national park which is lusciously green and features some of the oldest trees in America, beautiful giant Redwoods (which we missed as we drove into the park so we had to take an 80+ mile round trip to go back to the start again. So worth it!)

It's definitely lightning, I saw a bolt from the sky connect with the mountain top in the range ahead. Mixed with awe is the fear that we're in a metal box driving toward where it's striking every minute or so. Being in Death Valley is like being on another planet, like the 'Mars scene' from Total Recall just before Arnie's eyes explode. The RV is holding her own although you can't put your feet on the ground in the passenger side as it feels like there's a fire under your toes.

There are so many risks of death in the RV that I'm surprised humans are allowed within a 2-metre distance; like one of those fenced off electrical boxes you see on a street corner. These dangers are multiplied by the act of driving through one of the most inhospitable places on earth.

Ways we could die...

- *Death by being blown over a mountain side – I've been surprised & thankful to meet 'Sensible Sam' on the* treacherous corners, a personality of Luke's I have not come across before. I've been very impressed by Luke's road skills, unlike at home where I was counting the days for him to sell his car due to his erratic driving.

- *Death by Massive Explosion* – At gas stations we have to turn a lever to switch off our pilot light, sometimes we forget to do this. Just yesterday as we were filling up with flammable gas a woman smoking a cigarette came to ask if our RV was 'pretty tight inside?'.

- *Being boiled alive.* It's an oven on wheels with an engine. It's 112 °F (44.44°C) outside and we've been warned that Death Valley is the hottest place on earth. Our RV company does not allow driving through Death Valley in July & August. They refuse to extend insurance cover for the hottest months. Luckily for us it's September (just) so we should be completely fine! The hottest air temperature ever recorded in Death Valley was 134 °F (56.7 °C), which is the highest atmospheric temperature ever recorded on earth.

- *Turning things on in the wrong order,* a massive no – no apparently. Never turn the generator on when the Aircon is set to on. This is a little difficult to manage as the air-con buttons do not correspond to their labels at all. It's like they want you to fail!

- *Running out of water* (an oversight on our part and nothing to do with the RV) we drank milk instead. If we had broken down we would have 4 Budweiser's and a tank full of our 'non potable' shower water. We're not sure what unpotable means but it does not sound tasty.

- *Death by exposure.* Because you've driven through Death Valley *with a tank full of your own excrement the smell and the heat makes your demise via running off into the desert seem like a sweet escape.*

- *Death by spousal manslaughter because he will just not put the SEAT DOWN usually not a problem but seeing as his electrical toothbrush and iphone6 are precariously placed on a shelf just above the chemical abyss and I got the blame for being 'clumsy' for once knocking said toothbrush off its inch square topple-prone base I'm a little tense now.*

- *Death by knockout, when you've gotten out of your seat, and seatbelt, to fetch your overheated, dehydrated boyfriend some chilled almond milk and he takes the corner at 60mph.*

- *Death by lightning... I could go on, but we haven't read the manual fully.*

I laugh to myself as I remember reading 'make sure to have plenty of water' as we share our last cup of milk." We're getting on well considering we've condensed and combined our lives into a 25ft rattletrap box. We bicker for about 30% of the day BUT we laugh, love and cuddle too. It's not like it was at the start of our relationship, a year ago when he didn't snap at me and I wasn't an whinging-arse-bag but we still cook for each other and try to impress each other with plans like we did in the very early days of dating so we are very happy to have met, planned this adventure and to be living our dream.

When we have time to reflect, which is rare, it's a miracle that everything has fallen into place the way it has and we have not been killed by the RV, or each other, so far.

Mick refuses to pay for our camping spot as there is an honesty box rather than a manned kiosk. It makes me feel very uncomfortable not paying. Luke reasons that no-one is going to come and check, I look around and there's nothing for miles, no sign of life at all. I decide to hand wash some clothes and hang them out to dry in the heat of the night. Instead of going back inside to argue about the use of honesty boxes I lay down on a picnic bench just outside our metal box home. It's dark and the stars are all out. I can see them so clearly as there is no light pollution. It's a relief to stop for a moment and reflect on where we've got to.

LAS VEGAS

15th September 2017

I insisted on driving us into Vegas, I wanted to experience the strip from the road. I was not disappointed! Luke had never been before and it is one of my favourite places in the world. I came for my 30th Birthday with my Mum and Auntie as part of a Country Music tour we paid for using inheritance from Nannie after she died. It was a soul lifting mecca to Dollywood Tennessee and we all loved every second.

My Auntie Karen did all the driving as my mum was scared to drive or let me drive. Mum has a knack for finding every dead end on any given route while walking so we didn't waste time allowing her to attempt to navigate out of the hotel room more than once. Organised and capable Karen was our saviour. Before this trip with Luke I always left the planning and navigating to others, my friend Zoe is an itinerary queen, our short European breaks always ran like clockwork and we fitted loads in. Zoe would include designated 'fun time', all activities at a reasonable cadence, plus tea and cake stops were central to the day's plan. Leaving Luke to create a plan was dangerous for my health. I preferred my method of going with the flow without much of a plan but during our 2 weeks in America our time was limited so I gave in to his request of a little structure. As we drove into Las Vegas, I pointed out the different hotels, and we made our way to the other end of the strip so we could see the 'Welcome to Vegas' sign. My family & I had missed this last time as we were on foot and often exhausted by the long-distance walking and weary from the rum and coke we carried round in chilled little flasks. The RV was a good move in terms of transportation to the sign; 'Welcome to Vegas' was a picture opportunity not to be missed. We parked up and it felt so good to get out of the van after the long drive and feel the heat of the Nevada sun. The atmosphere in Vegas felt light and joyous. I was shocked at how much I loved it here. Last time I came was 6 months after I had been to India for the first time. India, then, was my favourite place, a place to see the realities of life and death, celebration and colour, it humbled me and made me re-think everything about my comfortable life in the UK. Vegas is the opposite of India. Nothing is real, everything is an advert of the real thing. Helicopters took people on destination-less joy rides, expensive drinks, shows, parties, it's all a front. India has no front, it's dusty, real, dirty, where kids live on the street, here, kids are celebrities performing on stage. Las Vegas showed me balance, it was the Yin to the Yang and rather than seeing it as a wasteful, I felt it as a luxury. I loved both equally and felt grate-ful to be a tourist of the two polarities.

BECCA BLOG - SHOE SHOPPING

16th September 2017

"We've been travelling for 6 weeks now, and I haven't worn heels in all this time. I've packed only flats so I won't be wearing them in a while. The transition from wearing make-up everyday has been a smooth one, my skin is much nicer after I've spent a few days in the sun. My short hair has gone a funny shade of ginger but that's ok too. The lack of heels and nice clothes has been a bit trickier for me. Everything I've worn for 46 days has come out of a crumpled; often smelly pile which has been squeezed into a compression sac.

The glitz and glamour of the Las Vegas casinos has led me to the ultimate dress up box – Sarah Jessica Parker's first and only shoe shop. In the Bellagio. SJP played Carrie Bradshaw in Sex & the City – my one time role-model; New York columnist & fashionista has a shop full of beautiful footwear!

The shop is quite intimidating for someone wearing cycling shorts and a bag featuring a Canadian-Maple-Leaf emblem but I wanted to feel girly if only for a minute. I told myself I would try on a pair of shoes. I choose some sparkling blue boots that are about $500 and I expect the shop attendant to ask me to leave, but once he's served another lady who looks like she is serious about actually buying shoes he comes to me. I try not to feel bad and decide I will buy a mini perfume for his time. I toy with the idea of telling him I just want to feel glamorous rather than a happy camper but decide *against it.*

* * *

While driving into Vegas I saw a sign for 'Dining in the Dark' . It reminded me of a romantic film I'd seen where two people fell in love over dinner just by talking, they couldn't see each other. I researched the restaurant to discover the experience would be completely pitch black, the servers would be wearing night vision goggles.

We found the 'Oasis' park to hook up the RV for it's much needed water supply and at just $42 a night it saved us some pennies over the big hotels. We had a swimming pool and hot tubs plus a laundry room, who needs the Bellagio!? We booked an Uber to take us to 'The Blackout' restaurant which I decided would be my treat. As we walked towards the door we could both smell sewage, not a great start but we went in anyway. After a short wait in the brand new reception area we were led through two fire doors which kept the light out of the main room. The waiter led us to our table by a sort of conga line as we couldn't see anything. I worried about having a panic attack but mainly I was excited about the food. I had read that your taste buds are heightened when you can't see the food. We discovered that deep fried vegetables dripping in fat taste pretty rank, the first course was not what I was expecting for the $100 I had prepaid for the 'experience'. The courses didn't get better from there and I was actually glad I didn't have to see the food as well as eat it.

I left Luke to plan the rest of our time in Vegas. We only had three nights before we had to drive to Los Angeles. Naturally; he wanted to do *everything*. This itinerary was for one evening, not that I was aware of half of it before it started as Luke wanted to keep it as a 'surprise'.

·   Steak & Cocktails at The Mirage.
·   Circ du Soleil Beatles show at The Mirage.
·   Ride on the Ferris wheel (High Roller) at The LINQ.
·   Upgrade the ride on the High Roller to include unlimited drinks for $40 each.
·   Giant Jerry Springer style argument on the strip.
·   Helicopter ride over said strip.

All this had to be squeezed into a 5-hour window. It was an evening we'll never forget but for all the wrong reasons. We barely made it to the last Helicopter ride and when we did, we were exhausted from the stress and arguing. Our evening started off well, we had a gorgeous steak meal, Luke's cocktail came to the table in its own smoking glass wardrobe which was very cool. The steak at $50+ each deserved to be savoured but we literally had to shovel it into our mouths and run to the show. We realised as we rushed to be seated with minutes to spare that Luke had booked our seats for the following night. We would be on our way to LA by then, to return the RV, so we naturally panicked that he'd lost the money he'd spent on the 'Beatles Cirque du Soliel'. Vegas being Vegas, this was not a problem for the lady at the desk who gave us tickets to that night's show so quickly and efficiently I wished I was travelling with her instead. Luke had the audacity to ask if the seats were still good ones!

During the show Luke sent me to get more drinks to 'make the most of it', the show turned out to be quite short so I spent 10% of it buying two alcoholic slush puppies for $30. We somehow navigated to the Ferris wheel after the show for a 30 minute ride which Luke insisted we upgrade to include a free bar for $40 each! So basically he chain drank rum and coke for half an hour – encouraging me to drink quickly to 'get our money's worth'. Drunk, we had to get to the Heli-pad that Luke had limited details of. We had to find an Uber pick up point which is not easy on the Vegas strip with no Wifi. We ordered a few that we frantically searched for as the time ticked on past our slot. I was exhausted by this point so we had a massive argument coming down an escalator of a plush hotel. There were people all around but I just didn't care and we both yelled at each other really loudly to an audience, I was so pissed off that we had to rush around so much and that way too many things had been planned badly. This was the reality of Manic Micks planning, Luke had good intentions but had got carried away and I was drowning in tides of stress I couldn't escape from. It's hard not to sound ungrateful, I am grateful for the helicopter ride which Luke paid for, as well as the majority of the other experiences that night but, I would prefer a little less stress.

I asked him to plan only one or two things a day from then on and never to plan 5 massive things in one night. This was the extreme nature of our relationship. The Helicopter company agreed for us to have the last tour of the night. It was incredible, terrifying and flying towards and above the brightly lit casinos over the strip was an experience that will stay in my mind forever. Another guest was a man who had survived cancer, he was taking the flight with his wife as a celebration, but he was so scared he kept his eyes closed the whole way. I was scared too but felt I should embrace it. Feel the fear and do it anyway, but like our relationship, it wasn't easy. I felt if I could open my eyes to everything that was going on I could allow myself to feel the good and the bad. I thought I would get some brilliant memories, learn lessons from the bad things and have (hopefully) some interesting content for this book! In stressful times my mantra was 'it will be good for the book'.

The following morning we had to be up for 5am. I was hoping we'd make it to LA to drop off the RV by 11am.

A BRIEF VISIT TO LOS ANGELES

We arrived in LA with minutes to spare to drop off the rental before we incurred a late charge. Miraculously we made it. Neither of us are religious but on the forecourt 9 days ago we prayed to God that this trip would go well. We were both well outside of our comfort zone. I had been absolutely terrified of driving the big RV but now that fear was replaced with a bit more belief in myself and it felt good.

Ever the wheeler/dealer; Dyno had the idea that we could get some money back or at least avoid being charged extra when we returned the vehicle, because of course, we'd gone over our mileage. I agreed it would be a good idea to mention our issues, being as that morning as I emptied our toilet via a black plastic hose they supplied I found a hole in the side of it. Dyno embellished the story to include us being covered in our own shit, which worked! In LA they were happy to feel superior to their San Francisco office by cutting our bill down to £0 owed.

We went to a bar that night to watch the boxing match between Canelo and Triple G and shared a cab with R & B artist Jordan Morris from the UK who was just releasing his first single. We made a point of sharing cabs to see who we met. We went down the walk of fame. I wasn't sure what I was expecting to see but an animated fight between two half naked street sleepers, followed by one of their arrests probably would have been last on the list.

The next day we got on the bus to Venice beach. It was strange to have to rely on public transport again. We tasted the best Fish Tacos and we got new backpacks to replace the PE bags we picked up in Newark! The idea behind them was that they were easy to pack flat into our bigger bag but they weren't easy to use as the draw-string cords would cut into us. Our new hippy patchwork bags felt a lot comfier.

GUATEMALA BLOG

18th September 2017

"We've arrived in Guatemala in the rainy season which runs from May until exactly the 1ˢᵗ November. The Mayan calendar is so exact that our Guatemalan Host Leshe and Irish partner Helena have never known it not to finish on the 1st of November every year. Like us; Leshe and Helena travelled the world together for a year when they first met. He said when you travel together you either love the person or you hate the person. They have now settled down with their two year old son in Antigua, Guatemala. Leshe carries an old backpack covered in the iron-on badges like we've just begun to collect and Helena is relaxed, slim, friendly and beautiful.

On the roads the drivers communicate like bats in the dark, there are no street lights, often car headlights don't appear to work as a pair. There are people running across the road wearing all black, tuk tuks weaving in and out between the cars and chicken buses passing like shiny metallic circus rides. Apparently the roads get even more dangerous uphill as the fog is so thick you can't see more than a foot ahead. We saw one bit of flat land today. The hills are a luscious green, and everything grows well here, including the beans for the best coffee in the world. I saw about 4 dead dogs by the side of the road but plenty were alive, roaming the streets. This is the most foreign place we've visited together and we both get the feeling our trip has really begun. We were a little nervous about Guatemala, especially when neither of us could remember why we wanted to include it in the first place. A quick Google and we remember it's because of the mysterious Mayan ruins which cover the whole of Latin America. We want to learn about the Mayans.

As it turns out; Guatemala has coffee, rum, chocolate, tortillas and guacamole to boast about too and that's just what we've discovered in the first 72 hours."

*

* * *

Antigua, a city in the central highlands of Guatemala, is a town so beautiful and cobbled that it's on the UNESCO world heritage list. We got talking to a Danish guy called Jonathan, on a rooftop bar who mentioned he had climbed one of the 37 Volcanoes which surrounded us. He showed us pictures of marshmallows being roasted over an open hole in the ground. 'We have to do that' I said, and Luke agreed. Jonathan was studying Spanish and his school led the volcano tours. A tour was planned for Saturday with space left so Luke booked us on. The hike turned out to be a 4.5-hour climb up the biggest hill you can imagine covered in thousands of years of black Volcanic grit. Of course Luke was in his element while I was a solid 10 minutes behind everyone else apart from a young girl from Rotterdam who had possibly not experienced a hill before, seeing as Holland is flat. I was slow but I enjoyed looking at the forest canopies overhead, although when it got steeper near the top did I get a little fed up. Luke had taken the contents of my bag to save me the weight and gave me his walking stick so I now had two yet he was still at the front despite carrying double the weight!

The climb was worth it and we spent time watching a giant Volcano erupt with Lava every 30 seconds through the night. Explosive thunder burst from deep inside the Earth. On top of Acatenango we had a view of 5 other volcanoes including the active Fuego and Pattaya (where the marshmallows can be roasted) and 3 others in the distance! The view we saw is on the cover of this book. The experience of being on top of the volcano was other-worldly, it's something we would never have experienced if we had stayed at home. Safety rules didn't seem to exist in Guatemala. Twelve people had died a few weeks prior to us doing the same climb, apparently they had gone without a guide, bad weather came in and they died of hypothermia while attempting to descend in the pitch black. Nine months after our night there, 62 people were killed and 300 injured. Dozens of communities were buried when Fuego spewed a 5 mile high lava stream into the air. This was just one of many of our brushes with death.

It was freezing in the tent the night of the hike and rain poured through a hole in the canopy above our heads. We shared our tent with the lovely Dutch girl, most of the tents had four people in so we were relatively lucky we weren't overcrowded although there was still no spare room. We were hoping the extra body might provide extra warmth but we were perishing. I'm not sure what kept me awake more, the erupting volcano, the cold or the rain dripping down onto us. I felt very ill for a week afterwards but the experience was worth it. When we were up the top we discussed with others how risky this trip was, we reassured ourselves that if something was to happen, it would be a good way to go.

Guatemala: Where shitting your pants and getting rabies are the good parts.

Luke diligently wrote profiles for us on a global volunteer website called workaway.info. He spent hours in the evenings researching and messaging hosts that needed a personal trainer (him), social media marketeer (me) or both. At short notice he found a 6 week placement in Santa Cruz, in a small community on Lake Atitlan, Guatemala with 'Amigos de Santa Cruz'. This not-for-profit improved the lives of indigenous people there by running a school, café and artisan shop. We would be getting free accomodation, $10 a week food allowance and free food from a café which overlooked the lake and volcanoes. We were excited. It was an amazing opportunity to be part of a different way of life and to give our time to a great cause.

 Lenny had messaged Luke saying he could do with marketing support for 'Amigos' and his wife Emily needed a personal trainer. The school turned out to be incredible but Emily didn't actually want a personal trainer.; she wanted a divorce from Lenny. We spent a week with Emily as Lenny was away in America. That week we barely left our gorgeous little open plan apartment. It had two double beds, an outside kitchen, our own bathroom and an incredible view of the lake. As I was recovering from the night on the Volcano we slept in separate beds but as the week went on we continued to enjoy our own space! What a difference from the night in the tent. Here we even had a TV and a DVD player. One morning we woke up to the sound of bagpipes, I couldn't believe what I was hearing. We walked to the bottom of our garden and on the pier that jutted into the lake was a Scottish piper fully dressed in his kilt, sporran and crisp white shirt. We spoke to Ross who told us he was on Instagram as @thefirstpiper. He turned out to be aiming for the world record of playing bagpipes in every country in the world.

I'M GOING TO SHAVE MY HEAD

It had been on my mind since I saw the rage in Britney's eyes as she smashed up her partner's car. She escaped the appearance that everything was as perfect as her airbrushed album covers. I didn't have the music career or looks of Britney but I had achieved what I *thought* I should but I had slowly realised none of it was making me happy. I wanted to travel the world and be creative but first I had to learn to let everything go.

I wanted to make the ultimate statement to my ego: that I no longer cared what I looked like. I want to be free of how I thought I should look. I thought shaving my head was the 'fuck you' my ego needed to let other insecurities go. "Look I don't have hair – deal with that!" I imagined feeling beautiful without hair, stripped bare. I wanted to take away all the places my ego resides in order to be free of it. In this freedom I hoped to become closer to my true self. Conveniently Emily was a hairdresser, she thought I was mad and tells me about how she used to drape her long hair over herself and her husband when they used to have sex. I headed to the salon, which was a shed at the end of the garden. She added that in the Mayan tradition if a woman is raped they will shave all her hair off. That makes me want to do it even more to show there is strength in being bald. I realised they were her fears surfacing and projecting onto me. I brush them off and my hair goes with them, down the river that flows underneath her garden room and into the lake. Luke shaved my head and was very supportive. I looked in the mirror and it didn't look as bad as I thought it would. I look content, empowered, happy, playful and fearless. I hashtag my picture on Insta #baldchicksrule. I've fulfilled another life-long dream and defied what all my friends said, I just went for it. I was learning to trust my inner self and not worry about what others think. It was empowering. I told myself that as my hair grows it will be a metaphor for my life. When I gave up everything (material) to come travelling I didn't know what would happen, when I shaved my head I didn't know if it was going to be a mistake. I trusted in impermanence. Things might be bad, they might be good, I wanted to work on my inner self.

DEAR FRIEND, THERE IS A DIFFERENT WAY

21st September 2017

 With a lot of spare time and a renewed sense of confidence in what we were doing I wrote a letter to a friend.

You are thinking of travelling, longing to hit the pause button on your life, to reset, to find yourself & begin again. You've worked so hard for so long, School, College, Uni, now you've been employed for 12 years straight, you've got to where you wanted to be, but you wonder is this it?

You and your husband have a car each to drive to jobs which pay for your mortgage. Sometimes you feel like cogs in a machine you want to turn off... if only for a little while. You created this life, you thrived on the pressure of climbing the career ladder & achieving the goals you had set.

In Secondary School, we went to 'Careers Guidance' together. This was exciting and scary, it gave us a glimpse into our future & with a pinch of self-believe we chose what we would be when we grew up. The next step on your path is children; but the stress on your body from your career is not allowing nature to take its course.

You're frustrated, you carry on regardless, too afraid to make such a drastic deviation to travelling the world, you've invested so much into what you have right now.

I look back and wonder why 'Volunteering at a Kayak Adventure

School on a remote Guatemalan Volcanic Island' wasn't presented as a clear option to us aged 15? Travel is not as expensive as you think it is. You could move to Vietnam tomorrow and cut your living costs by 75%. Advertising by holiday companies makes you think that travel comes at a premium when in reality if you planned it yourself you could save thousands.

We put our flights on an interest free credit card and pay just pay it off at £82 a month. What could you cut out to afford £82 a month?

You & I lost touch after school to fill you in on a few things that brought me to escaping the life I had created:

- *I wanted to travel at 21, but at 21 I got my dream job of working for a newspaper, after I did my Journalism degree. I tried to do TEFL (Teaching English as a foreign language) alongside my first few months of my career but it was too hard for me.*

- *At 21 I made my first attempt at settling down with a boyfriend, owning furniture & making a home. It failed, I did this again at 23 & 28 with increasingly disastrous results.*

- *The 28-year-old attempt ended because my boyfriend turned out to be very bad news, the relationship was on and off & during an 'off' period I'd booked a trip to India. We'd got back together & rented a beautiful historic cottage which we filled with IKEA furniture. While in India I realised I'd been emotionally abused since we got together & that one time he was violent to me was really not ok. India showed me I didn't need any of the material possessions I'd worked so hard to amass. I landed in England feeling very different, feeling that if I only had a roof over my head I would be in a better position than the majority of India (I saw) who have nothing. He knew I was different & wrecked the house, but only the things I had bought back from my trip strangely!*

I picked up my work laptop on the way out of the door and slept on my friend's sofa for a month before Women's Aid re-homed me.

· *Once I settled into my new flat with beautiful cream carpets, a balcony & across-the-road access to a 24 hour McDonalds I had this massive fear of this 'being it'. No-one could understand & I went into an existential crisis. From the safety of my new flat I could see my Uni apartment where I'd started in Lincoln 12 years prior.*

· *I found Kundalini Yoga brought me such relief from work & life stress. In a strange experience during a private lesson I saw myself as her in the future. She lived with very little possessions and was enviably happy. One friend who met her for a minute & experienced her light and happiness said 'I really need to do yoga if that's what it does!'. I wanted to be that happy too.*

· *I met Luke. This was the biggest catalyst for change for me. Luke had wanted to travel for even longer than me. He wanted to leave for world travel 7 months after we met! I wasn't ready. I was scared about leaving my job and not having any money, about whether I could really do it. If it wasn't for Luke's support I wouldn't have been brave enough.*

· *I read a book called 'May cause Miracles' by Gabby Bernstein. It allowed me to believe that miracles will happen to you if you believe they will.*

A book called 'Get Rich Lucky Bitch' by Denise Duffield Thomas made me think differently about money. I realised I didn't have to stockpile it, it comes and goes, you will have enough as long as you appreciate and are grateful for what you have. It's very 'Law of Attraction' so I recommend you read 'The Secret' first. Believing that the 'universe supports your decisions' and 'whatever you think you become' required a massive shift in mind-set. I.e. from work hard, knuckle down and you may have a couple of holidays a year until you retire.

· *I saw a 'Past Life Regression therapist' if the advice above was too woo-woo then it only gets worse from here! Any kind of holistic therapy should help with your stress but Yvette at Red Hall Clinic Lincoln really took me to the next level. I hadn't finished reading 'Get Rich' so I said to Yvette a couple of times that I couldn't afford it at £75 a session, Yvette advised that I need to be 'aware of the messages about money' I am putting out to the universe! I had three sessions and my confidence in following my dreams was through the roof.*

· *I quit my job. This was by far the hardest decision. I just couldn't believe I could do it. Luke & I had a trip to Istanbul which was so eye-opening & we both just came alive travelling. In bed on our last night I told myself I had to start my own business and leave the job that was keeping me in one place.*

I hope this inspires you to take the action that I know is bubbling under the surface for you.

Lots of Love

Becca xx

* * *

I had searched for the most romantic place to take Luke for his birthday while we stayed at Lake Atitlan, Guatemala. El Artesano Wine and Cheese Restaurant was reccomended, in San Juan, a town famous for native artisans working in handmade traditional crafts like weaving and beading. It sounded perfect. Two people had told me about the restaurant; the manager of the school we were now volunteering at and Lenny, but neither of them had actually been there. I had ordered a birthday cake from the kitchen of the school, using Google translate, "Pastel manyana por favor", despite a few Spanish speaking lessons and using the free website Duo Lingo I hadn't learned enough to add real urgency so I waited a few days for the cake to materialise!

I had bought my love a big bottle of the local Guatemalan rum; Ron Zacapa, plus a new top and I had printed out some messages from home and a picture of us on top of the volcano. I got myself a new dress for about $10, a little too tight for my western body and pattern looked like it had orange nipples sewn on it, but I felt in the mood for celebration regardless. We were all set for a birthday adventure.

Luke likes a solid plan but as it was his birthday I was in charge of the day's events! The day would be a surprise to me too being as I had only booked the table, everything more would be down to chance. So far, the universe had been on our side, and we were beginning to feel that the world was made to be explored.

We had time to burn before lunch so we walked into the garden of a house with an old 'tourist welcome' sign outside. There was nothing inside to see, we reasoned that whatever it had been, perhaps an art gallery, had closed some time ago. A lady hanging some washing out came over to us and explained something in Spanish, she beckoned us to follow her. We weren't sure whether to as we had no idea where she wanted to take us! Still in good spirits we followed her through dog-shit strewn alleys in the blazing heat. At least this way we avoided the trucks full of carbonated sugar drinks that had left barely enough room for us to walk along the roads. We reached a coffee plantation that her son, an artist, was finishing building. This was to be a new venture from the old one we'd walked from. The man kissed and thanked his mother explaining to us that he was an artist and he would love to show us around and make us some coffee from the beans he'd grown and show us his art.

His paintings decorated the walls of his café where we could try the coffee he grew. We ate the coffee beans straight from the tree which were delicious. Aside from getting bitten by some ants, trusting and following the old lady had paid off. We both loved exploring that area of the lake that day. Looking up from the streets we could see a mountain which looked like a person laying down, It was called the sleeping Indian. We planned a hike up there within the 6 weeks that we were to be on the lake. The wine & cheese restaurant was beautiful. Wild dogs waited outside for the best scraps in town. It was set in a garden with lots of native flowers and vintage French antique decorations. They had three delicious platters on the menu, we were told in advance the meat and cheese were not to be missed. A cat was curled up next to me on the bench and the place had such a warm feeling of relaxation and luxury and we were the only guests.

We gorged on cheese & pastrami platters and we ate the cake I had carried around all day and had pictures taken by people waiting for their boats. On Lake Atitlan; boats are like buses, picking people up from piers. There were tonnes of boats but we weren't aware of the scheduling, we were about to find out the consequences of my lack of research! Walking towards the pier to catch a boat home it started raining, rain in this area of the world means darkness descends and the streets turn into rivers. The wind really got up and we dashed into a shop to help them cover all their stock that was getting soaked from the sudden heavy downpour. We didn't really want to order a drink as we had been wandering around drinking cocktails for a few hours after lunch. We had drunk at least one bottle of rosé between us and were nicely tired and ready for bed.

We explained we were just waiting for the rain to pass for the next boat, a young girl in the café, a customer, overheard us and said that the last boat had just gone. Surely, they wouldn't go in this rain I thought, although perhaps it was safer on the water in a monsoon. The land was basically steep hills leading toward a volcano crater filled with water (the lake). The owner confirmed that the boats had in fact stopped. No more boats! We were stranded on the wrong side of the lake, in the rain and the sun had now set.

We quickly learnt the Spanish for boat; 'Lanter', we kept repeating this and the destination but there was no hope. The seemingly haphazard coming and going of boats turned out to have a strict shut off time. Whoops. Cold and wet with the novelty of the day wearing away, we agreed to get a tuk tuk to the next pier. It was now pitch black. The tuk tuk had no window wiper but it had its own flapping raincoat with floor to ceiling slits to let the pouring rain in. Huddling in the back seat we started the journey around the hillside, there were no roads or street lights, just dirt track. I clung on to the horizontal rail that separated us from the young driver, it was covered in plastic like a coiled up spring, its indent soon marked into my gripping hands. We had considered staying the night at the artisan town but I had some work to do and we wanted to save money. In my mind it would be a good end to the day to be warm in our own beds. This Tuk-Tuk journey was the definition of treacherous, the whole of Lake Atitlan is volcanic, the 'road' was black gritty stone with giant potholes. We had a really tight deadline to get to the next pier before it closed!

Stressed and scared we got to the pier and the last boat had gone. Gutted.

Our only option was to go by private boat and the last one of those was about to leave. It had cost us about $2 for half the distance this morning, but now we were going to be charged $30. I just paid and acted like I was happy to do so for Luke's birthday. I felt this was my fault for not checking the return journey times. The boat ride was interesting, some boats we had been on had a roof, this one had a boat-length sheet of blue tarpaulin which whipped every few seconds. Luckily the whipping only took 5 minutes, making it our most expensive journey so far but worth every penny, we were back to our beds with a lesson learned, and a lovely day had.

* * *

Not deterred by my mishap with the boat times we planned another trip to mark the last day of our 6-week volunteer project. I had finished my social media training for the young women in the artisan workshop; they could now confidently promote their weaving and beading products on Instagram. Luke had a filming project to complete so I set off down the steep hill toward the track back to our house. Tuk-Tuks came up and down the hairpin tracks of the hillside all day, a couple of them stopped and asked if I wanted a lift. I always got a lift up as the hill was a pain in the arse but down-hill I could manage, and the sun was out. After refusing the second lift I heard barking, there are loads of stray dogs in Guatemala but apart from the tonnes of shit, I had not had a problem with them until now. Two dogs came running out of a house, and onto the track I was walking down, really angry, really barking, and I was scared. One dog seemed crazy angry that I dared to walk past, I still debate with myself now whether it was 'rabies angry', as before I could run away, it bit me on the back of the leg. FUCK! I threw my water bottle at the dog but missed, I got a jog on, my heart was pounding and I was terrified of Guatemala again, was this dog going to chase me all the way home and maul me to death? I should not have walked alone but I didn't think of the danger of dogs. Ironically their territorial nature also saved me as they didn't follow me further than a few metres away from 'their land'. I got back to our place and our hosts said it wasn't deep enough to turn me rabid. I was afraid that I had rabies none-the-less. After a few hours at home I was still worried, I wanted to go to a clinic for the rabies shot.

Later that evening I walked to meet Luke for a drink with the Amigos team, armed with a 'dog bashing' stick, until that day I had wondered why people were carrying sticks. I had heard about gun crime here but not the leg biting canines. We had just not read up the particular dangers of this central American country but then our research was limited to pointing to a place on a map.

Luckily someone knew a nurse and I was able to discuss with her about the rabies shot. Unfortunately there were none on the lake and I would have to order it in at a cost of £88 per shot, and that I would need 5 shots! I would have to travel to the nearest city and wait 3 days, as it was revolution day, a holiday. All that time negated the need as I would probably be rabid within 4 days. The bite had hurt but it wasn't bloody, could rabies have entered my skin through the tiny puncture wound? Did it matter that my rage-red mosquito bites looked much worse than the dog bite? Maybe I had malaria too and this whole trip was just a bad idea.

My mind was racing, some rum helped to slow it down. Luke was going quite strong on the Jack Daniels too so we relaxed and decided to get a boat across the water to a place where we had loosely booked some accommodation for the weekend. We were planning to trek up the beautiful mountains that looked like the 'Indians Nose' we had seen from the restaurant on his birthday.

If we had known the literal shit-storm that awaited us we would have just ordered some more drinks and stayed for the much talked about drag show. A drag show seemed wildly out of character for the area but I can't say any more about it as we were on our way across the lake on the last boat before it was due to start. So far our Airbnb experiences had been good but we had yet not received an answer from the host where we had booked and paid for that evening. To bide our time we found somewhere to eat which looked quite cool, all seats were on the floor and more sleeping cats curled themselves into decorative cushions. We ordered some food but after waiting half an hour we were told the chef had gone home! I can only assume that the waitress didn't speak English so didn't feel confident enough to tell us we were never going to get our dinner. We were using the 'restaurant's' Wi-Fi to message the host, hoping for a reply so we could get checked in but nothing was working out for us. We had the address, so we decided to attempt finding it via Google Maps. In rural Guatemala there are no street names but there are mud tracks, boggy fields and alleyways. If you are lucky you will be walking on a potholed pavement teaming with rabid dogs, I had learnt the hard way not to do this now. We got a Tuk-Tuk which we directed from the backseat, the driver had no idea where we were talking about, nor did we really. We searched through corn fields and in the end realised it was hopeless and the host likely wasn't going to be there anyway. We were going to be out of pocket but on Google Maps we could see a 'hotel' nearby, so we looked for this instead, I found it eventually, at the end of a farm's field behind a gate! The 'hotel' we found was actually a few sheds, an open-air kitchen and a chef who only cooked bolognese so we ordered it, despite Luke starting to develop some stomach issues likely related to stress and the parasitic water of Lake Atitlan. We enjoyed the bolognaise and were shown to a room, 'basic camping' described our digs, but it was $15 and we were completely lost and stranded so we agreed. The room had a broken TV straight from the 60's and a bed. There wasn't much room for anything else. I spotted a giant Spider which our new host promptly beat to death, quite a prolonged murder which Luke and I just watched, lacking the energy to step outside, or language to suggest just chucking it in the garden would have been ok. The bed only had a thin sheet, not for us but for the mattress, perhaps as guests we should have provided our own sleeping bags. Luke's guts were getting worse, he rushed out to the loo and I closed the door behind him, big mistake, we were about to realise.

With Luke a lot can happen in a small amount of time. At home in Newark he would often come back with an elaborate story which I couldn't believe he had the time to fit in, minutes since I had last seen him. His brain injury really does have an effect on his day to day life. We had both been out drinking in Lincoln and decided to carry the party on at his friends, 20 miles away. We left our cars in Lincoln, the next day his uncle took us to fetch them and we drove back for Sunday dinner at his Nans. Pure bliss, a hangover cure of a Sunday Roast and doing nothing, I got the Sunday paper and settled on the sofa, waiting for him to arrive, he was just behind me, from the same place so surely, he won't be long. As I wait, his Nan got a call, Luke's explaining on the other end that he is at a garage in Lincoln and can't pay for the fuel because his card is in his back pocket and the zip has come off! Apparently, even the petrol station attendant had tried to get into the pocket for his debit card with no avail. The manager had been called and three grown men debated and tried to get into Luke's pocket for his card. Luke had decided he liked the shorts too much to use scissors on them! He finally came through the door and his Nan easily got the pocket open while Luke instructed me to go and pay for the fuel for him the next day!

In Guatemala a similar spectacle unfolds while I witness it all in disbelief. He had run out in his boxer shorts and was now trying to get back in, but the door wouldn't open. I was trying everything I could from inside. He was apparently trying everything from the outside, but I later found out he had his underwear in his hand as he had shit his pants before reaching the toilet! Someone had been in the loo, and his stomach was not in a good way. Now he was naked, trying to get in a door which wouldn't open and yelling at me from the other side. God knows why that door didn't open but 10 minutes later it just came open and wasn't a problem for the rest of the night. We know because

Luke was up and down until the sun rose. I watched his colour change from green to grey and he didn't look in a good state at all. As the night went on, it was clear he was severely dehydrated. I needed water too as we had been drinking at the pub before we left the other side of the island but we had no water with us.

Trying my best to be a supportive girlfriend I said would get something for our thirst. At dinner I had noticed a camp-bed that suggested the host likely lived in his kitchen. Our shared dining table was propped up against a large fridge, all the on-site facilities were quite compact so I knew that the owner's supplies would be in that fridge and it was our time for some good news. I vowed not to come back without water. We would be hydrated and on the road to recovery for our hike the next morning. I walked through the garden towards where we had eaten dinner. As soon as I pulled the table from in front of the fridge scraping the heavy legs on the concrete floor I heard him coming out of the door. I didn't expect the machete he was wielding but I had practised in my head, 'Lo Siento, Agua por favour': I'm sorry, water please! I showed him the water, which I would be taking no matter how much he waved his machete around, and I trotted back to the cabin. I was elated over these cool waters as they were our first positive achievement all day, they were large bottles too, cold and delicious, I was so happy!

By the time morning came, the colour of Luke's skin told us that we would have to abandon the hike up to the sleeping Indian and go back to our own luxurious apartment with two double beds and a fully equipped kitchen. Why did we ever leave?! We settled our bill for the room, dinner and water amicably and luckily didn't see the machete again.

❊ ❊ ❊

Lenny and Emily often had guests coming and going, we didn't think too much about the three new people hanging around our kitchen that morning. It became apparent that they had stayed over in the spare apartment, three of them in a small room because they had needed help at late notice. One American guy, a German guy and a girl from New Zealand. They had met up the day before to go on the 'Indian nose' hike which *we* had planned to do. Terrifyingly they had been held up at gunpoint. Robbed of everything they had on them, they had lost all their money, bags and passports leaving them just one credit card between them. Some men in a truck had stopped them as they started the hike and fired guns into the air, easily convincing them to part with their backpacks. We realised that we would have been victims too had our plans not changed. All of a sudden I realised everything we had been through, the dog bite, Luke shitting his pants, the last minute 'hotel' stay and our consequent return back to base had saved us from being robbed or worse. We would have left most of our valuables at the Airbnb (if it had worked out) so the gunmen may have reacted differently to us. A few hours later we heard from the guy who owned the Airbnb and he was full of apologies and offered us a place to stay there anytime we wanted! We also got a £90 credit on our account. This taught us that when everything falls apart it's not always a bad thing, it could be saving your life.

A FINANCIAL SETBACK

My client base was made up of old clients which I had at the paper and who I'd built a great working relationship with over the last 9 years. One regularly paid for the service wanting not much in return but her social channels to be updated regularly. I never thought I would have an issue with this client, until she emailed me saying they had sold their company. I didn't see it coming, I lost £400 a month just like that. Then two more followed suit in a similar fashion, one didn't see the value in what I was offering and another had major cash flow problems. In just six weeks my business I was left with £800 a month. I imagined it was doable to travel the world on £800 a month, bearing in mind our flights were already paid for (albeit by credit card!). Losing more than half my income that early into our year was a shock initially but I sat by the lake and thought about what I could do. We had a free place to stay here so I would just have to take it a month at a time. This month would be ok but we would have to make a plan for the next month. I still had my savings and when that ran out I had my overdraft. I drew on my sales experience and thought about how I could get more money in. I spoke to the clients I had left to see if there was more opportunity and within a couple of weeks I had secured another £200 bumping up my income to £1000 a month. I was keen for work not to be my focus as it had been for the previous decade. So the extra time was welcome. I was on a search for freedom but having lots of clients meant I had to be at my laptop everyday for a few hours.

Unfortunately the worry I felt around losing my remaining clients cast a shadow on our days. I made myself so stressed with anxiety that my remaining clients would leave me that it would have been better for my mental health if they did. Around 8 months into the trip I lost the extra £200 a month which really took the edge off my worrying. I had gained a new client by this point, my first client who took me on knowing that I was travelling the world for a year. I hadn't admitted to my clients that this was what I was doing. I was worried they would think I was on holiday. I regularly insinuated I would be back soon, knowing that I wouldn't be. No wonder I was anxious! I spoke briefly to a mindset coach online, she encouraged me to 'own' what I was doing, so what if my clients thought I was on holiday? I still couldn't do it. My own facebook posts were hidden in a group of 200 family and friends. I did show on my page my work with the Mayan school where I was teaching social media but overall my channels showed little of the magical things I was experiencing because I was worried about losing my precious income.

SAN MARCOS

Blog 28th September 2017

"I'm studying for my Reiki Master qualification this week.

Yesterday I was introduced to a symbol that heals at soul level. According to Katherine, my teacher; the levels 1 & 2 sort you out mentally & emotionally but this one is the BIG KAHUNA! - (Sorry I'm also reading a book about Hawaiian shamanism.)

After this course, I will be able to attune other people to GIVING Reiki. This is great because I love to help other people become who they want to be. I followed my calling to the 'Holistic Cottage' San Marcos, Lake Atitlan, Guatemala' & now I have a massive smile on my face because I know I'm meant to be here right now. Sometimes during the process of becoming a Reiki Master, there is a healing crisis, Reiki is a powerful healing energy from the source of the universe and if something isn't right with you it will bring it to the surface. I had over an hour of Reiki by Katherine at the end of our first training session which revealed some issues. As Katherine held her hands over my upper back my heart started pounding with an anxiety feeling. It had something to say.

The whole time I was laying down my uterus was killing me. I'd had mounting gynecological problems since the emotionally abusive relationship a few years ago. I felt pains there as I laid on the treatment bed. More came up in my mind's eye when Katherine worked on the back of my body than anywhere else. I could feel the energy on the backs of my legs. According to my teacher; 'what's be- hind us in life affects the energy behind us'; it's symbolic of some-

thing pushing you or pulling you back. Katherine said I 'present' that everything is ok but there is something deeper, another level that's in my past that's holding me back from being completely healed. At first I think; I have worked hard on forgetting my past, I don't want to bring it up again, I want to forget about it, but on the other hand I want to learn from it and use it to help others. In the past, abuse has not been spoken about, it wasn't long ago that it was ignored by society in marriage, and tragically it still is in some cultures. The recent #metoo campaign is a change I want to be part of. I told everyone who was close to me about what happened to me and most had their own stories of abuse at the hands of previous partners, parents and even grandparents. I wasn't alone. Katherine told me I have a glitch in my second chakra, this chakra relates to blame, guilt, money, sex, power, control, creativity and ethics and honour around relationships. Physically if this chakra is out of balance it can manifest in gynaecological problems, pelvic pain and urinary problems. I have been experiencing problems relating to the second chakra, since 3 months into the bad relationship. I realise that although I'm totally fine with not being in the relationship anymore I hadn't grieved for another loss.

I never recognised on a deeper level that the day I left him; I also left my step daughter. She was 6 and so beautiful. The joy that little girl gave me and the power of the love I witnessed was literally life changing. When I heard her Dad talk about how he held her when she first came into this world made me want to have kids. I had never wanted children that seriously before. When we broke up, I went to the family planning clinic to get the 5-year coil to ensure that I wouldn't get pregnant. I think on some level I believed that me wanting children was a result of his brain-washing and that really; I did not want children.

After the coil I had a smear which came back showing abnormal cells which could turn into cancer if not treated, after the treatment I passed out as it was quite awful. I know now I need to *journal and do the emotional work around this. To make a start, I wrote a letter to my ex-stepdaughter (that I won't send!) just for therapy. I forgive him for the way he treated me as I understand he is just a product of how his parents treated him.*

After a massively transformational week; I feel like new.

I've become a Reiki Master!

* * *

My week with Katherine came to an end today at a sacred hillside Mayan Ceremony space overlooking the ancient mystical Volcano crater.

Katherine chose the place for its energy, the energy of Noj, the 13th Mayan symbol. I discovered a little about the Mayan calendar here & mainly that my sign is the very same! Luke had brought me back a little hand-painted canvas of Noj after telling an artist my birthdate on our 2nd day at the lake .

On the way to complete my attunement I stopped on a rock to take a photo, as my ceremony finished & I was being taught how to perform it for others, a giant bird started circling above - picking up the wind streams that had stirred up above us. Then the same bird was waiting for us on the rock as we walked back! It looked like a vulture so I'm hoping it took away all my negativity that I've had Reikied & massaged out of me this week. Yesterday I journaled for hours working out what I am to do now I have this qualification & I came up with exactly what we are doing now, traveling, writing, working as a creative, cooking great meals and just living the lives we dreamed of when we were back in the UK. Luke did a course this week too and is now a qualified Thai/Yoga massage therapist so HAPPY, HAPPY days.

MEXICO: THE DAY OF THE DEAD, DRINKING PETROL & OUR CHILEAN HOST'S ITALIAN RESTAURANT.

1st November 2017

By the end of our time in Guatemala we couldn't wait to get away. I had thought seriously about leaving before the end of our placement as the tension between our hosts was so negative. We were brought in as a plaster on a wound that ran very deep. Such a beautiful location and perfection in photos but in reality, the love was gone, and it was sad.

Amongst the collection of DVDS in our apartment was the latest James Bond film, featuring a few scenes in Mexico at the Day of the Dead celebrations. I had been reading about how Mexico celebrates this day around the time of our Halloween by visiting their lost loved ones' graves, however since the James Bond film 'Spectre' was released mass carnival-type parades had begun. Life was imitating art. In Guatemala we were relatively close to Mexico (by our estimations anyway) so we looked into flying there for a week before we were due in Panama.

We arrived on November 1ˢᵗ to discover, once we got to the town square, that the 'Celebraciòn de Muertos 2017' started on the 28ᵗʰ Oct, we had missed the parade. We could however see some of the floats displayed. We had picked our Airbnb based on our hosts, they were our age and were up for showing us around. We met Angelica and Milo when we arrived late on our first night in the country, not forgetting Sheera, their little ball-of-fluff dog who greeted us with many loud yaps! It was Milo's birthday, so we had picked up a bottle of red, which turned out to be a perfect choice, Chilean, as Milo was from Chile and this was his favourite wine. Luke claimed that was the reason he picked it. Angelica was studying and working as a nutrition-ist yet made us all hot dogs out of a jar and rolls out of a bag, possibly the least nutritious food we had eaten recently! We weren't complaining though after a long day of travelling it was lovely to be fed and we enjoyed some birthday cake along with the wine. The after-dinner tipple of 'Mescal', a 41% proof 'drink' tasted like petrol, but we had plenty of time this week to get used to it.

We always like to wander around a bit round the streets to get our bearings and familiarise ourselves with the neighbourhood, after 3 months travelling, we had become pretty fearless about being in new places. 'Mexico City' rang a distant bell in my mind of somewhere I had been warned about. We learnt from Guate-mala though that fear of a place can be unfounded and anyway my fear of Guatemala didn't stop me from being attacked by a dog! We passed a couple of stunning women in skin-tight, short electric-blue dresses standing by the roadside with two litre bottles of water close by. We realised these were working girls, out in the morning, this perhaps wasn't the most upmar-ket neighbourhood. We nipped into a shop to get an ice-cream, that's when the trouble started. Luke got a pink ice lolly while I went for green, so far so good, but as I bit into mine I discovered it was full of spicy brown sauce. Luke's had a sweet strawberry centre, normal, while mine was one of the worst things I've ever tasted. Spicy ice lollies were a first for me, my mind was blown. I tried to 'empty' out the sauce by holding it upside down, but I could still taste it, needless to say Luke didn't want to swap with me. Milo explained later that it's a Mexican thing, to add spice to everything needlessly. We needed to watch out for this.

Travelling full time meant that we were together more often than not 24 hours a day. Even though the majority of the time we got on each others' nerves we continued to live like this, due to habit, and being so busy that we couldn't really carve out alone time. Thankfully Milo had offered to take Luke to a football game while Angelica and her friend Rosa would take me to a parade. With Luke gone I felt a little sadness and worry that he would be ok, I told myself it was healthy to have some time apart as we would have something new to discuss with each other when we met up later. We got started on our night ahead and made head-dresses from orange flowers while Rosa gave me a choice of traditional outfits. I spoke as much Spanish as Rosa did English but girly nights seemed to be universal, make-up, Mescal and a night on the town needed no translation. We went back to the square where Luke and I had arrived on our first day and the place was transformed, swarms of people, ghouls, clowns and candy-skulls were queuing to get on a free bus tour of Mexico City. I'd never seen so many people in my life, all in good spirits! There were lots of children amongst crowds despite it already being quite late. Some clowns were so scary that children were crying! It felt amazing when someone stopped me to take a photo of my make-up, I had used my liquid eyeliner to draw a candy skull on my face and against the orange flowers it was quite a look. I was flattered. No more worn-out traveller face, I was paparazzi fodder. To top off the night there was an English translation to the bus tour I listened to on headphones as we were taken around the city full of parading spectres. Tacos were our midnight snack as we made our way home, exhausted but what an experience. Luke had enjoyed his visit to the Azteca Stadium, made famous by Maradona's 'hand of God' goal.

To return the favour of our new friends' hospitality we decided to cook them a traditional English roast. Luke's piece de la resistance is the Yorkshire pudding, AKA that's his total contribution while I do the rest. The roast potatoes, Jamie Oliver style chicken with a lemon unceremoniously shoved inside plus vege. Gravy was impossible to find so I made a sauce from tomato puree and vegetable juice. Angelica was shocked at my daring ability to light their dodgy oven, with a match, while she usually burns a long piece of paper.

While Angelica watched me cook in the tiny kitchen I was telling her about how we lived our lives, she was telling me how she wanted to travel but had schooling to complete. I got the impression she didn't feel passion for her life. Her partner didn't like Mexico or the Mexican people, he spoke in fondness about Chile while Angelica reminded him that last time he was there a policeman stole his phone. Dinner was a hit, our hosts were impressed. Milo's comment of "Masterchef" as I put his plate down in front of him remains one of my proudest moments.

On the other hand, I will always remember nearly dying there. I was standing on the bed by a body size open window and reached up to hang some clothes onto the curtain pole. The bed was the exact height of the window. It was dangerous and stupid for me to be hanging things up there, but we had needed somewhere airy. If I had fallen out of that window it would have been too high to survive. Every morning the building shook as big trucks went by outside. I felt shaken thinking about my possible death. I heard that when you face death you are more grateful for life, but when I think about that window, I just feel uncomfortable and cringe at how stupid a death it would have been, death by laundry.

Milo owned and ran a small Chilean/Italian craft beer & pizza bar, these really were the perfect hosts. For our last night we enjoyed a meal of delicious calzone and cheesecake followed by an evening of drinks with a big group of their friends. I was tired but someone had a pipe so Luke wanted to stay and party. Remaining loyal to fearlessness in the face of the obvious danger I got an Uber home on my own, to a flat I could hardly find during the day, plus my phone had no battery. Not my smartest move putting all my faith and life in the hands of an app. Luckily it paid off and I got back ok. After a week of partying, beer and Mescal I was ready for a detox.

In Guatemala I had discovered famous people who share my mayan birth symbol (Noj) and one of them was Frida Kahlo. Frida was a Mexican self-portrait artist with a tragic and colourful life which she portrayed beautifully in her many paintings. She's a Mexican treasure and the first Latin American female artist to be recognised internationally. I became obsessed with Frida and finished a book I paid £28 for on her life story. She cut off all her hair once when she found out her husband had an affair with her sister.

* * *

On a day away from Mexico City, we visited the Teotihuacán, Sun and moon worship pyramids. There were some amazing ancient wall paintings preserved. I gleaned from the visit that centuries ago people came from all over South America to meet here to exchange tips about agriculture and water power. The sky was a bright blue and the pyramids were stark and brightly lit by the hot sun. We often took the same photo on two different phones so I put my phone away and enjoyed being in the moment, letting Luke take the photos. Unfortunately for us we never saw those pictures again. We had been warned about pickpockets operating on the 'metro' underground and had been told to wear our backpacks on our front and try not to look too touristy. On the way back home, buzzing from our day trip we forgot all these precautions and paid the price. As we approached our train, it was packed, two armed police got on the carriage to the left and we chose the door to the right, in hindsight maybe we should have followed the guns, but my instinct was to avoid them. As we stood up on the train I worried about being groped, on a previous journey Angelica had explained that women have their own carriages for safety in Mexico. I looked at Luke, the epitome of tourist, shorts, sleeveless Tupac vest with a hood, a blue patterned 90's bandana, wearing his pack on his back. The bag it turned out was not the target but the phone in his pocket was. As a group of people left the train, I saw a piece of paper that I recognised to be our colourful to-do-list that we often filled in to keep us on track of the week's plans. We realised then that something had slyly been taken from Luke's pocket. The carriage was emptier than before but there were still plenty of people around, Luke didn't go as mad as I thought he would, but he was pissed off at himself. He couldn't really start accusing people as we were outnumbered and had no clue who had taken it. It was over very quickly with the note on the floor the only real sign anything had happened. Luke said later that a girl was looking at him, keeping eye contact, perhaps as a distraction while someone else went into his pocket as the crowd pushed towards the door. Very efficient and thankfully non-violent. By the time we got home the phone was wiped, we couldn't even attempt to 'find my iPhone' or remotely wipe it, the criminals were professionals. A few days later they were using Luke's Ebay account to buy more iPhones and getting Ubers all over Mexico! Uber was no help with sorting out the problem. I had to think out of the box to stop the thief getting lifts on Luke's account. I took Luke's card details off the app and added a card onto the account that didn't have money on so no more journeys could be booked.

FROM MEXICO TO COSTA RICA AND PANAMA

I got a taste of what it must be like for Luke living with his brain injury after a one night stopover in Costa Rica. When things like this happen I am reminded of what he has been through, how ill he was and I tell myself to cut him some slack. I like to think I do this every day, by being calm and patient but the truth is I have my own moods too and am not as understanding as perhaps I could be. I'm often busy being a moody bitch (Polly) when hormones win out. I became so confused about where we are and who our host is that I suggested to our Panamanian host to use the 'dog buggy' she told us about yesterday, but it was actually Gianni's dog buggy – our host from the day before. My brain is scrambled over dog transportation and covering three Latin American cities in 24 hours. I need a rest and thankfully it's coming.

Facebook Post - 7th November 2017

Today is already a better day than yesterday. Here's a list of actual events.

- We have to leave our new best friends in Mexico City.

- We're told to go to gate 25 and that's what it says on our boarding pass. We notice the sign on the gate says Bogota CO. I think this must be Costa Rica but Luke claims he knows that Bogota is Columba as he's seen it on a banged up abroad episode.

- Our tickets are checked and we are the next ones to board.

- Our names are called & we are informed that we are boarding the wrong flight! - The gate had been changed.

- We run to gate 29 - we can't sit together as the plane is full.

- We land in Costa Rica a few hours later & queue for TWO HOURS to get through security. I have a sore throat/cold and neither of us are impressed with Costa Rica airport.

- We try to get an UBER, the app has stopped working.

> *• We try to get cash out for a Taxi, I realise one of my cards is lost and the other doesn't work.*

- Luke manages to get 10,000 Costa Rican Colón out which is about £13.

- Taxi driver takes us to the condo, he can't find 62B after three attempts at driving round and going back to the guards at the front, we get escorted there finally by young armed guys on scooters.

> *• Taxi driver doesn't have any change, so we get into our second Spanglish debate with him & the guards.*

- After a lot of standing around shouting NO CHANGE Luke and the cab disappear, I'm left not knowing where he has gone and if he's ok.

- *Miraculously he then gets dropped back by the same taxi 5 mins later - he'd taken Luke to the shop to get change, tried to drop him at the main gate but Luke was having none of it!*

- Once we're inside the house the neighbour comes round as our host is on the phone saying the 'Police Woman' at the gate had said we had no money to pay the driver.

All ok in the end, we order a load of Sushi to be delivered and get an early night.

Back at Costa Rica airport now & heading to Panama to meet the lovely Ana Marie - a friend of Luke's who has an amazing week planned for us.

PANAMA

13th November 2017

From the moment we arrive in Panama we relax, Ana is there
to pick us up from just outside arrivals, no stress getting a taxi
or searching for somewhere to stay. We are in the car and off
to the supermarket on clear roads. Panama is hot and humid.
Luke met Ana a few months before we boarded our first plane,
she was in London taking part in the same teacher training
Boxing Yoga™ course. Thankfully Luke is really good at getting to know people and had told Ana, and her husband Pedro,
of our travel plans. They had invited us to Panama as part of
our trip. We filled a trolley full of food, keen to show our hosts
that we wouldn't turn up empty handed, unfortunately the
total came to $130, a big shock for us when just weeks before
we had been buying fruit and vegetables for pennies from old
Guatemalan women. Panama seemed more Americanised with
its skyscrapers and billboards. The streets, although filled with
nice cars and not a Tuk-Tuk in sight, were very overcrowded.
It seemed like the infrastructure had no way of keeping up
with the population. Ana told us that people had to leave their
homes as early as 3am in order to get to work because of traffic
and some people hardly saw their families.

We managed to keep out of the traffic to get to our home for the
week, a spacious modern apartment high above the city, complete with two of the cutest little chihuahuas. Having worked
in hospitality Ana was a natural host, we chatted about books
and she mentioned a book that my Reiki teacher had told me
about: The Artist's Way. I took it as a sign I must read it. The

Artist's Way is a guide for creatives to support them in birthing their ideas and living a more creative life. The author, Julia Cameron, recommends writing three A4 pages each morning, something I have done since that day. It helps me clear my mind and clarify any creative ideas that are forming. Julia Cameron and Elizabeth Gilbert (Eat Pray Love) have taught me that we all have a duty to bring the ideas within us to life, if we don't, they will go to someone else. Cameron teaches that it doesn't matter if anyone reads or enjoys your work it's all about the creation.

When Panama was created, millions of years ago, it appeared out of the sea and joined two parts of the world together that had never before met, this created a link from one side of the world to the other. The country is now home to 220 mammal species, 226 species of reptile, 164 amphibian species and 125 animal species found nowhere else in the world. Panama also boasts more bird species than America and Canada put together. Needless to say we saw loads of pretty birds. In England we can rely on my Grandad to identify any birds we see, we sent him pictures from Panama but he didn't have a clue! We stayed with Ana & Pedro at their apartment in Panama City then visited their family's country house for the weekend which was nearer the beach. This couple could not have made our stay better. We even visited a beach where it never rains & drank mojitos all day whilst singing songs from the musical Grease. Pedro played guitar back at the country house whilst we sang and drank Bacardi, playing Uno and enjoying another of our roast dinners. Bliss.

ANA'S STORY

"I worked in the hotel industry for 10 years, for Trump for 4, it wasn't what I wanted to do and it ended badly. I had no idea at 18 what I wanted to do with my life. I was on a work exchange from Panama to Germany, I stayed in a small German town & I hated it. I went to live with my uncle who eventually took me back with him to Panama but because I still had no direction I ended up going back and completing the year exchange. When I returned my family wanted to know what my career would be. I remember being at my Aunt's house and seeing a hotel out of the window & just saying 'hotels' my aunt rang my Mum and everyone was so happy that I'd finally decided my career. I nearly met Donald Trump once, he came to the opening of the hotel I worked at in Panama City. I was waiting ages in the foyer for him to arrive. I thought I would go and freshen up, I came back from putting lipgloss on and I had missed him. Everyone was like where were you? He was meant to stay for Lunch but he insisted on taking the lunch away. I was the purchaser for the hotel so I went out to get the best Tupperware & wrapping for him to have his lunch on his flight back to the U.S. While I was out there was a tropical rainstorm, the water got so high I couldn't get back to the hotel. One of the porters had to wade out and collect the wrappings. I went to my Mum's for the afternoon. I enjoyed working as a buyer for the hotel chain shops, but I was recruited into residential property management which was really corrupt. Two years ago I was in a bad accident with a taxi driver who was speeding on the wrong side of the road, he died. I'm waiting for a trial, he had a wife, there was a hearing and their lawyer said 'we want to sort this out' but I've heard nothing since. Due to the case I need to apply for a permit to leave the country

whenever I want to go on holiday. I went to London last year to do a Boxing yoga course. I've just qualified. I want to see more clients for health coaching & Yoga. I'm adding mirrors to my wall in my spare room for a studio but my Dad wants to help me create a retreat centre."

* * *

COSTA RICA

At the beginning of our time in Costa Rica Luke and I hadn't been getting on at all. Unfortunately, this coincided with Dawny, Luke's Nan coming to visit us, which likely took the shine off her holiday. We booked a week in a B & B we found online. From the pictures it looked like it was in a green space but that green space turned out to be a rather exotic garden in a really busy part of the city. We spoke to the owners who allowed us to cancel our booking for the next few days, leave our bigger bags there and move on, before coming back for Dawny's flight back to the UK at the end of the week. We made the best of it and went to the beach for 5 days via a tiny 6 seater plane. We joked about how nothing phased Dawny, the flight there was scary but she took a nap. At 75 she was fearless. To get to us Dawny had to travel via the London Underground, which she had never experienced before, she voiced her surprise to us that she hadn't had to walk through a 'Tube'. The three of us went on a Dolphin spotting trip, although there were no Dolphins in sight, there was a generous supply of alcoholic drinks to order. Luke and I wanted Dawny to have the best time and we wanted her to see a dolphin, she said 'bugger the dolphins' which we thought was hilarious and a great sentiment. After a lovely week of sunbathing and swimming in the sea we headed back to catch our return flight.

We turned up to check in for our flight to find no planes at the airport! We were told the airline was closed down by the Government during the time of our break. We wouldn't be flying back from the beach as we planned. For about half an hour we called the company we booked with, without much luck, we were worried we would be stranded.

Fortunately, a bus came to pick us up, it was comfortable and although our journey back to central CR was long, we took in some unexpected scenery that we would have missed had we taken the flight. Once back at the posh B&B we asked for our bags and they were nowhere to be found. Dawny had left her iPad and we had left a lot of our stuff too so we were panicking. The hosts started panicking too after realising the bin men had been the day before. I envisioned searching through a landfill somewhere but they turned up in the garage wrapped in black bin bags! The host was 80 years old and his memory wasn't the greatest. On our last night we ate steak at an upmarket Italian restaurant then the next morning said a tearful goodbye to Dawny.

PACHAMAMA, IN COSTA RICA

28th November 2017

We were finally getting near to Pachamama, the spiritual forest community/yoga/plant-based/cleansing/retreat. Yoga teacher had recommended Pachamama, she had been herself after seeing a friend who looked incredible, and asking her where she found that glow to her skin. They both did the '37 Day Transformation Course' that I longed to do too.

Luke and I made our way towards the retreat by staying a few nights in Nosara. There we enjoyed pizza after a day of bike riding. Of course we got lost. The bikes didn't have brakes, they were meant to slow down when you push the pedals backwards, this function seemed redundant as Luke came hurtling down a steep rocky path towards me shouting his brakes wouldn't work and stopping himself with his flip-flopped feet. Needless to say he wasn't happy. Hot, dusty, lost and arguing about which way we should go to find our digs, we needed this retreat more than ever.

My mum wondered what I would be transforming into as she already saw me as a spiritual yogi. By the end I had transformed my knowledge and mindset around food. For the first time in my life I felt empowered and able to make good food choices based on ethics, the environment and health. Rather than 'slimming or dieting' I finally felt in control of food. I went from 'Pug at a Picnic' to 'Vegan Vigilante' in 5 weeks.

We started our transformation course by doing a 5-day body cleanse. This included living on juices made for us from 100% organic local fruit and vegetables, twice daily enemas (self administered) in custom built cabins as well as daily yoga, group sharings and meditations. The first day we had a visit from the community's leader; Tyohar, walking his pregnant deer. Apparently, he had been given it after its mother was hit by a car near the forest. Tyohar moved here 25 years ago with his life partner, friends and the followers he had made as a DJ and spiritual teacher while travelling around the world. This place was becoming more and more interesting by the minute. The actual minute that we arrived into this seemingly silent and abundant forest Luke suddenly started swearing and jumping about. A scorpion had climbed onto his boot and up his sock heading towards his ankle. We made our presence known! Pachamama had fruit trees, bamboo, and tall shady canopies above giant tendrils of roots. Man-made and animal paths wove through the forest toward architecturally wonderful eco buildings. There was a school, a restaurant and small huts where the guests and volunteers stay. We were to stay in a 'casita' which was a three walled shedlike structure with just a mosquito net over the bed to protect us against the elements and howler monkeys! The shower was very basic and very cold and the nearest bathroom a short hike away! These were not our biggest concerns. Part of the retreat was to be 10 days in silence and we were both nervous about this. However, we had 20 or so days of other 'work' before that. The therapists and Yoga teachers there were world class, blending childhood regression, breathwork, nutrition and popular psychotherapy techniques. Spiritual and personal growth was the base for the healing journey.

One particular workshop was so powerful I managed to rewrite my childhood story; up until then I had been subconsciously telling myself that I was at a disadvantage from being in a single parent family. I was carrying this limiting belief that I had a lack of support and that was why I struggled with pushing myself out of my comfort zone. In reality I realised that I have an abundance of people who love me, including my Grandad, my other Grandad in the spirit world, countless family members and my real dad if I was willing to let him in. I changed my mindset after that 3-day course. Luke unfortunately left the course one day in. He switched to a yoga study. I felt that the course would have been good for him but he didn't want to do it. Although we argued a lot before we arrived, the retreat took the pressure off our relationship as we could hang around with other people our age. The structure of the course meant that we also didn't have the daily responsibility and debate over where we would be sleeping or eating. We wanted to heal our relationship and we were given the space to do so. It was at Pachamama that we felt our trip together had really begun (Only 4 months since we left the UK!). We wished we had started there as soon as we left England to set our year on the right path. As well as the community who lived full time in the forest and the volunteers, sixteen other people were with us on the course, we witnessed their transformations, their tears and sharings. It was beautiful to see people investing in themselves and healing from the inside out.

Throughout the silent retreat we sat and listened to Tyohar speak, these nightly meetings were called Satsang, which meant a 'meeting with the truth'. He was enlightened, so he had many inspirational and soothing words for us. The only way we could communicate through the 10 days in silence was via letter to him. This was so we could take a break from meaningless conversation and really 'go within'. We also weren't meant to be making eye contact with people. This began as a challenge in our cabin with Luke wanting to have sex 'one last time' on the night the retreat began. I wanted to take part in the retreat 100% from start to the end so he was left high and dry and being vocal about his perceived injustice. I felt it was a lesson I had to learn to stay silent against the odds. We paid a lot to be here, why retreat half-heartedly? I sensed it was going to be a real challenge for Luke but vowed not to let his challenge be something I had to break my silence for. I was on my own journey. Luke did stay silent for the most part, but being a rule breaker he did write me letters. My first letter to Tyohar was about guilt and forgiveness. In front of everyone Tyohar read a letter out from 'Rebecca', it asked 'can I really be monogamous'? My heart sank. Luke would think this was from me. My letter was actually about the guilt I felt over once deleting my Nans collection of photographs accidentally by shutting her old computer down too quickly. Guilt over no longer working full time was crippling me and old feelings of guilt, source feelings perhaps, had come to the forefront of my mind. I wanted to purge them so I included them in my letter. (which was read the following day.) That night however I got back to the cabin to see Luke furiously writing yet another 'illegal' note while I patiently waited for it to break my Zen. He was outraged that I had chosen this platform to share second thoughts about our relationship. He knew we had problems but he did not realise they had got this bad for me. Also – that if I wanted an open relationship, he would consider it. (Good to know, thanks!). I calmly wrote that there was another Rebecca on the retreat and I hadn't written the the words that had been read out tonight. I was sticking to the rules of no eye contact, but I could sense he felt relief and that he believed me. I didn't say anything about the open relationship comment, that could wait. Before the silent retreat a beautiful blond girl had told me during a sharing session that she really wanted to find someone to have sex with and then later walked into Luke's shower cubicle twice. Luke had asked her politely to leave, I thought it was hilarious and said he should have gone for it but I think he would be too worried that I would want to do the same with some wild man of the woods. We assumed that many people on the retreat were in open relationships. Free love and knowing you don't own another person might be important to some, but we didn't want to add more challenges to our relationship.

* * *

I first met Michelle when we sat down for the orientation talk at Pachamama. She was quiet looked like she would rather be anywhere else in the world. I was enthusiastic and excited to be there but once she told us her reasons for booking the retreat I felt like a fraud. Michelle really needed this course. I felt at that moment that I was somehow intruding on her pain, insulting it with my happiness. She had lost her husband in an industrial accident 18 months ago. This retreat was the first step to really letting the pain go. She had been working up until now and had just quit her job to travel the world. Where we had begun to travel to find freedom, Michelle began her search for a life without pain. The transformation we saw in Michelle in those 37 days was phenomenal. To me she began as a closed book, her face scrunched up with her pain, by the end her face was open, vibrant and her smile was beautiful.

During an intense workshop called 'Who is in?' loads of us slept in the 'OSHO' hall together for 2 nights and the time we were awake we would be asking each other "Who is in?". The set up was around 100 yoga mats with a cushion on each side. We would sit opposite each other for 3 minutes while asking the question 'Who is in?' keeping eye contact until the bell rang. We would then swap the listener for the speaker and retain eye contact again, face unmoving, not speaking when it wasn't our turn. We were a mirror for the other person's process that was all. Who was in? I dug deep at the question, I was a daughter, a friend, a girlfriend. I voiced it all to the ever-swapping mirror. One man looked exactly like an old boyfriend I had when I was 15. I had completely forgotten, up to that point, how badly he had behaved to me, he had been controlling, jealous, violent and he cheated on me. I saw that this first relationship had unfortunately echoed in a few other relationships in my life. For this to come to light while facing him was revelatory for me. I found it difficult to look him in the eyes. As I sat opposite my pseudo ex-boyfriend I processed the grief and drama of 15 year old me. I allowed the pain to come to light and be processed rather than dwelling inside me for another 16 years. I attempted to understand why I allowed men to treat me badly and celebrated how I had walked away from that situation in style (beautiful in a pink BHS prom gown).

Did he just describe my dream to me?

As I sat opposite another 'mirror' he began his analysis of 'Who was in' and his words freaked me out. He was explaining in detail a dream that I had the night before. Obviously there was no way he would know this as I had not spoken to anyone but he seemed to know it all the same. It reminded me of the time I had first seen a psychic medium at a party after Nannie died. I had taken a picture earlier that day of my new curtains and noticed two orbs on the photo – one stronger than the other, at different heights. Perhaps looking for reassurance I imagined these as my Nannie and her Dad who had passed away one week before her, my Great Grandad. I went to this birthday party and the psychic picked me out first, she said my Nan and Grandad were watching over me and that they were happy to see me settled in my new home. The psychic got hiccups, my nan had hiccups while at the later stages of her illness, through the hiccups she got out a name, Geoff, this psychic had named my Great Grandad. I never believed in talking to the dead before. After my message had come through I went to the loo and had a cry, I felt broken open, vulnerable to so much wonder and magic it was overwhelming. I daren't imagine that these sorts of things would happen but more and more often they did at Pachamama. For me it was a place to connect with the divine.

❋ ❋ ❋

As carefree travellers, plant medicine ceremonies were something loosely on our agenda, there was a 'Rock Night' at PachaMama for $100 a ticket. Before attending we had to go for a de-briefing about the 'medicine' we would take. I found out that some people were avoiding the rock night due to the 'drugs' but that everyone else could not wait for the event, us included. Ingesting Peyote, a mild hallucinogenic drink made from a cactus plant, during an all night rave run by our enlightened leader seemed like the next natural step on our path to transformation beyond fear. We napped during the day and arrived at the party area around 10pm. It was at a natural clearing in the forest by a beautiful river. The centre point was an incredible campfire to one side was Tyohar's DJ booth and on the other side was the Peyote station. The station would open periodically during the night for us but Tyohar had his own supply he was literally spooning into his mouth while chain-smoking rollies all night. The music was out of this world, the setting was unmatchable. Glastonbury 2009 was my favourite weekend in this life but Pachamama's rock night is a clear rival. It was sensational in every sense of the word. The medicine was very gentle, keeping us awake and receptive to the message of the music and the connection to the earth, fire and each other, without any side-effects associated with chemical party drugs. We were transformed into plant medicine converts through dancing round the fire all night long and bathing in the river the next morning. Luke and I danced together lovingly like we didn't have a care in the world. Two men had the responsibility of fire management and constantly arranged and rebuilt the fire all night. We were mesmerised when they decorated the ashes into an effigy of an eagle or a love heart. One friend even said that he saw the fire respond to the fire keepers energy as if there were a mutual relationship between the man and element. That was how good the medicine was! With no hangover, only a deep gratitude for each other and everyone around us the sun rose and we applauded Tyohar with all our hearts and energy. There must have been over 100 of us there in the forest but miraculously food arrived from the kitchen for us all, including frozen sorbet covered in dark chocolate and tonnes of fresh fruit. Luke had about 15 'bliss balls', sweet energy balls, while we watched another guy practise so much gratitude for just one chocolate treat that it was entertaining for us less enlightened beings who wanted as much free food as we could get our hippy mitts on.

BLOG - PACHAMAMA'S 18TH BIRTHDAY

Last night we danced bare-foot under the stars at Pachamama, to celebrate her 18th Birthday & the opening of the new 'Wild Treats' bar! (It serves pure natural chocolate in the form of drinks, cakes & sweets!) We had a toast of Sangria & some cake. Yesterday morning we took part in a Sweat-lodge - for the 2nd time - there must have been 50 of us all sweating in a hand-built clay lodge singing songs & making the OM sound - pure bliss - the idea behind it is to offer your sweat to the Earth to show gratitude - the best part is crawling out covered in mud to wash & float your hot body in the cool river!

The therapy...

I had heard of 'primal scream' therapy, I imagined that you think of something and scream about it, that way you get the emotion out where it may have been trapped before i.e. as a child maybe you were told to be quiet so you never expressed your rage. This week we did some screaming in our 4 day workshop, we also hit things with foam batons that the Americans called 'Noodles', we drew child-like pictures with our non-dominant hand and created drawings from dark memories which we ceremonially burnt in a fire-pit. On day 6 of the transformation course I sang 'Thank U India' by Alanis Morrisette acapella style to 20+ people, so this week I was ready to put myself forward in front of 10 times that many people, to ask a question to Tyohar! The beautiful, glowing goddesses of the forest who live & work at Pachamama have names such as Tanmaya, Amari, and Rosana – Rosana looks like an angel crossed with Sandra bullock and Liv Tyler, from what I can decipher the R is pronounced as a HA – Ha-Sana… We are encouraged (on a Spiritual path) to accept serendipity but I suspected they weren't born with these names, even in a magical forest one has to ask some questions.

I wanted to know about the naming/ renaming process, I'd heard a few stories, like Tyohar used to give out the names at the end of the Transformation Cycle (that we are a part of) or you only get a name if you live here. I wanted to hear straight from our leader and use my new found courage to speak from the heart. (Everyday during this cycle we are 'sharing'; we spoke about our feelings and process, what we've taken from exercises, what we loved or hated.) This has become more natural and less terrifying over the last fortnight. Now, two weeks in, I'm finding it a great resource, it's incredible to be given space to share. Someone said today' "the space between doing and not-doing is as thin as the thread of hair". I resonated, I have said for a bit that I'd love to do a workshop on singing or sounding (from humming to primal screaming) but I've not done anything about it. I feel it's a massive thing to host a workshop and I'd need the right logo, branding, acoustically accommodating space etc. I realised today; I could ask a few people over to our casita, sing a bit of lady gaga and talk about our self-expression, AND BOOM, I've made the first step into "doing"- rather that procrastinating and creating such a worry around the imaginary 'workshop' that it never begins. I asked my question about the names. In a very eloquent, inspiring and thoughtful way Tyohar said I 'trumped' him, he'd never been asked this question before and didn't know how I 'found out' about the names! He said it's not encouraged but we can request them, mostly it's done after your 3rd visit here but there is no set rule. The women in the group intuitively choose your new name and Tyohar whispers it to you or possibly hands it to you on paper. I want to ask for one. Someone *else said you have to use it or give it back. I was thinking I could use it as my Reiki practitioner name and my singing & author name but what the hell, I may as well just try it on for size for the next 8 months while we travel then see how I feel: "Hi I'm Arangor son of Odin." Before I asked the 'trump' question I spoke about how I felt, for the first time in my life, that I can sit and relax without 'doing' anything, just 'being'. I told him I'd never felt so alive and so relaxed at the same time.*

There was space yesterday to express our gratitude at a beautiful altar of OSHO's picture, (OSHO is Tyohar's Master and when alive he was a mystic, guru, and spiritual teacher from India.) I had a profound experience that I was on the right path, that everything in my life was playing out as it should. I heard OSHO say 'Yes' very loudly. I knew it was his voice from recordings I'd listened to. I knew then I didn't have to rush into running workshops, write my book or somehow define myself. I had been worrying about how I should tell people I'm a singer, Reiki Master, Social Media & PR, Author/ Travelpreneur but now I realise there is no rush to define who I am or do EVERYTHING RIGHT NOW.

Tyohar is a wildlife photographer, DJ, community founder and spiritual leader, and has helped tens of thousands of people heal. He's not wasting his time defining a Facebook or LinkedIN post to promote that, he is just being these things. He is letting his light shine in whatever way he feels & his creation (Pachmama) is celebrating its 18th birthday. I take inspiration from him today to 'JUST BE'. After all that is what my company brand is! (Just B Energy & Just B Social) I have to take some time to Just B me, in the forest.

✳ ✳ ✳

By the beginning of January we were both ready to get back on the road, we'd stayed at Pachamama for almost 40 days. During the retreat we had been eating a vegan diet. As we both looked and felt at our best we wanted to carry that on. Our optimism ended once we reached lunchtime on the first day. We were back to the poor Costa Rica that so contrasted with the community in the forest. It was unreal how they had managed to get that fresh food daily when outside you could barely find a healthy meal. The only place we could find to eat at was a greasy spoon café, while we waited for our bus to the main airport. Luke developed a sickness and diarrhoea bug before we boarded. The bus was overcrowded and we had to sit on the floor for 6 hours in the slowest moving traffic imaginable while Luke burped up increasingly horrendous smells of yam burger. I'm pretty confident neither of us would have survived that bus journey without the mindfulness we had been practising. Luckily too, Lorenza, a lovely lady on the course, had given me some baggy trousers. I would have been wearing a short dress the whole way which would have been even more uncomfortable. A large American 'Peace Corps' volunteer shared the less than a metre square floor space with us. It seemed like Costa Rican bus drivers favoured the locals' tickets over us tourists. Eventually Luke and I got a seat for the last 20 minutes of the terrible journey but the woman in front of me laid her seat right back into my space, laughing. I pretended not to notice, but it seemed obvious as tourists we were not welcome. If tormenting me brought her joy, so be it, this bus journey was normal to them whereas I knew we could go back to the UK and never have to sit on a dusty bus floor again. What an end to our retreat, I felt out of my depth, I wanted to go back to the forest where everything was peaceful and good. It was a shock to be out into the real world but we had the tools to choose peace, and it was up to us to integrate this into our lives on the road. The things that had transformed us were out of reach as soon as we left the community, in a meat eating, noisy third world country we had our work cut out.

TOWARDS MACHU PICCHU

3rd January 2018

Our first drink of the year – a pisco sour, was lovely. Usually our Christmas & New Years' would be a mess of alcohol and over-indulgence but this was the complete opposite – we were feeling nourished and whole. Lima was like most central American cities but there were a lot of pictures of the Pope. We were staying with a young couple, Christopher and Kevin, Chris was from England and had just been back there for the holidays. We got to sample some of his Nan's Christmas-cake, and we snuck a few 'Quality Streets' out of their tin. They still had their tree up with wrapped presents underneath as with Chris being away they hadn't had a chance to have 'their' present exchange yet. It was very romantic. Our room was lovely if a little small. There was a gym downstairs and Luke wanted us to train together. I used a gym once at Uni but since then I have not been back. I'd gone through stages of trying things like Cross Fit, Strong Man, and stuck to boot-camp a couple of times a week for a while but in the last few years I really favoured gentler exercise and the occasional Parkrun. Luke likes circuit training, hiit, and repetitive hard impact stuff that I really hate. We clashed over exercise almost daily, he has to do it for his mental health whereas I enjoy leaving it. Eating out every day was not keeping my number of chins down but we often walked over 10,000 steps a day so I wished he would lay off asking me to 'work-out' with him.

I had a client's work to do so I agreed on a short 'circuit', but I really have a short fuse listening to him telling me what to do. With every weight and lunge I was getting more frustrated. Surely this isn't enjoyable for him either I thought, he often says I'm the hardest person to 'train', good I thought, I'm not a dog. I left him to it and went back up to the flat, to the sanctity of my laptop screen. 'Sitting on my arse' Luke would often say. Well, yes, as that's the only way I can keep the keyboard on my lap. He really is infuriating sometimes.

A LITTLE CLOSER
TO THE RUINS

6th January 2018

We land at Cusco, a city in the Peruvian Andes and it's freezing cold. We delayed leaving the airport in favour of sampling the Coca tea, the 'elixir of the Andes'. Friends and family who have been to this part of the world, said it will really help with altitude sickness. It's made from the same plant as cocaine and it's illegal in alot of places but here they sell it in gift wrapped packets. Luke's looking a bit pasty, and I'm in need of bed. For once Luke doesn't want to rush into negotiations with taxi drivers, although this might be related to the fact we have not yet found somewhere to stay. I think back to being in England before we set off, when being in a foreign country with nowhere to sleep for the night scared me. Today we have not given it a second thought, the effects of Pachamama keeping us in the moment. The elevation here is 3,399 metres above sea level, 500 metres lower than the volcano we climbed last year. It is Luke's turn to choose somewhere to stay. We have begun to take turns at picking and paying for a place so we are not doing the same research at the same time. As a Libra, Luke likes to weigh things up, research all the options available and make an informed decision. I however will book the first place that looks decent, has decent reviews & that I can afford. If I get a good feeling about it, I'm sold. As Luke deliberates over tiny details I often feel frustrated and want to hurry him along. Especially if we are tired, hungry and have all of our stuff to carry which is pretty much every few days. Our personality types clash when something needs to be done. I'm the Ram, he is the Scales, channel the Ram I say, as he asks me to help compare his top three choices. "Ok so we have one with no water, one with no windows & one with no Wi-Fi". 'No water' I say, 'we can buy some and hopefully we'll get a discount on the room', forgetting about our need to shower. Cusco is rural, rocky and we see snow-capped mountains in the distance. We are here to make our way to Machu Picchu but aside from the well known picture of the ruins through the clouds we have no idea what to expect from Peru. We had no background knowledge on the country aside from our visa requirements. Luke talked to the Uber/taxi drivers and asks where the best places to go are, what we should see, where we should eat. It's more fun than a guide book and we left our lonely planet guide to the world in Pemberton, Canada, it was heavier than a house brick and nearly double the size!

In Cusco the streets are busy, there are school-children everywhere, and walking in the road isn't safe because the traffic is busy. We learn to be patient, no one seems to be in too much of a rush. The town square has a sort of 'out of season' ski village feel to it, the architecture is impressive and overall Cusco is very beautiful. We are well catered for with our new vegan status and enjoy a gorgeously decorated dish of fresh mushroom salad with edible flowers. We've come a long way from the Canadian delicacy of Poutine; AKA cheese chips & gravy!

Lots of men with stalls dot along the pathway polishing people's boots. I looked down at my own in judgement, they were looking scuffed and neglected, dehydrated from the Costa Rican sun. I wasn't sure about the currency, the language and didn't want to get ripped off. I decided to ask a lady boot polisher by gesturing at my boots. I check how much it is and she holds her 3 fingers up – 3 Peruvian Soles; 64 pence! This is the first time I've got them cleaned since we started in August last year, it's now January and I'd worn them most days. The lady was so skilled that they came up looking better than new, I was so happy I could have cried, what a difference it made. I gave her 10 soles – about £2.34, the least I could do. Her hands were stained black from doing the daily work. I hoped she could treat herself to something that would make her feel as good as I did right then. I floated to the cobblers for the final cherry on top, some replacement red laces.

I first replaced my laces after reading 'Wild' by Cheryl Strayed. She hiked the Pacific Crest Trail, 1100 miles alone at 27. My Grandad always had red laces on his boots too. Combined with a £6 pedicure a world of difference was made to my outlook and I vowed to take better care of my feet and boots from then on. We made sure we had a pedicure once a month, Cheryl lost 6 toenails on the trail and I wanted to avoid that. The next day the water still wasn't running in our Airbnb, our host had promised it would be, Luke had been helping her bring buckets of water from a giant well up 6 flights of concrete stairs. The room was cold, dark, and the other guests left all their dirty plates in the sink rather than using a bucket of water to wash them up. Like a few of the hosts we encountered this lady seemed to live elsewhere so wasn't available to help us much in terms of places to go and things to see. One night we got locked out and had to wait outside in the cold for an hour for her to come back, not ideal. In the end it turned out we were just using the wrong key.

I loved to take pictures of the local women and the children playing board games. One group of three young boys reminded me of little old men, they looked so wise and beautiful. Often, I would try to take the pictures without people noticing but a few times I asked, and they would happily oblige, or ask for money which I thought was fair enough. There was a time in the past I had been too afraid to ask for or take pictures of locals but it made for much better photos. This afternoon in the market, the stalls were so colourful and full of interesting products, most of which we had trouble identifying. One stall sold soap, cheese and caviar, with a mummified goat skeleton framing the offering. All the stalls were stacked like giant pyramids and the seller, a lady, was perched in the middle on a platform, strikingly stoic and unsmiling.

We managed one hot shower before we left our questionable accommodation for a trip towards Machu Picchu. As we stepped out of the door and onto the pavement a bus stopped for us and we hopped on, perfect timing, it was meant to be. All we had was a leaflet with some drawings of old ruins on and a few names in our mind who Chris, our host in Lima recommended; Sacsayhuaman because it sounded funny and Ollantaytambo which felt good to say too, anything else we discovered on the way to the main event was going to be a bonus.

The Peruvian landscape was shockingly stunning, I thought to myself that I must tell people to come here, why didn't I know more people who had been this way? Why had I not heard about the mountains, the snow, the culture, we loved absorbing it all. Our bus stopped at a place called Chinchero and we decided we would hop off to explore. The area, although quiet, turned out to be a regular tourist stop. At the top of a hill of cobbled stone we were greeted by a young lady in a red and black layered traditional dress who asked us to come into a walled area for a demonstration of something! Other young women were dressed the same inside, they seemed like young girls but we noticed that all the women were quite small here. We had a full demonstration of the process their wool takes from Llama to jumper including washing, weaving and dying. The demonstration was free but we were encouraged to buy some goods at the end, not that we needed much encouragement to buy brightly coloured handmade gifts. The traditional red woven fabric was offered to us to dress up in too. At first, we had been apprehensive about being taken advantage of, but we were having fun, Luke looked great in his funny hat and cape. We were even shown how to swaddle and attach a baby sling to my outfit which was heart-warming.

As we learnt about the coloured dye and where each colour came from she held out her hand and showed me two live bugs: "this is where we get the red colour", "Please don't kill them", I said although I was wearing leather boots and some alpaca wool socks I wanted to draw the line at killing bugs for a demo on Andean lip stain. She crushed them anyway and I was reminded of my work as a sales person, I always wanted to show all the features, facts and benefits to get my sale. This young woman was good at what she was doing, she wanted to be thorough. I didn't rub the red bug juice on my lips although I admitted it looked good on her. I was grateful to move onto blue which came from less violent sources. We noticed a small mock-up of an old village in the corner of the yard just as a couple of guinea pigs made an appearance there. Our guide explained they eat guinea pigs here! We had wondered why there were a few stuffed at the market in cellophane. It's good for protein, she explained. Their home was a mini palace, strange to be housed so well bearing in mind they were food, but I knew then why the little pigs were so skittish.

While in Cusco I got an interview with an online platform I found via a friend who ran her own business in Lincoln and promoted herself really well. I gave the answers below.

WHAT IS YOUR PROFESSIONAL TITLE?

Creative Marketing business owner who can sing at your wedding and give you a Reiki treatment.

WHAT DO YOU DO ON A DAY-TO-DAY BASIS?

When there's Wifi I manage creative marketing campaigns via Facebook, Twitter and LinkedIn for clients based in Lincolnshire. It turns out there is Wifi everywhere! Most days are spent trying to

balance discovering a new city & running my business which is a dilemma I strive to be grateful for everyday.

WHAT DID YOU WANT TO DO WHEN YOU WERE A CHILD AND WHAT CHANGED?

At 12 or 13 I wanted to be a hairdresser, I considered being a lawyer and then decided I would be a journalist.

WHAT'S THE BEST CAREER ADVICE YOU'VE EVER BEEN GIVEN?

No-one will think any better of you if you work through lunch.

WHO IS YOUR ROLE MODEL AND WHY?

Frida Kahlo the Mexican Artist, she painted her truth and didn't care for anyone's opinion, she was courageous enough to paint herself with facial hair, including the iconic mono-brow. She reminds me to be my authentic self.

WHAT IS THE BEST THING ABOUT YOUR CURRENT WORKING ENVIRONMENT?

That it changes almost daily! I've worked from a hammock in a Costa Rican forest and now I'm in Cusco in a lovely little kitchen cooking some black corn on the cob. I have a second hand Macbook I bought for £400 and it comes with me everywhere.

WHAT WOULD YOU CHANGE ABOUT YOUR DAILY WORK ROUTINE IF YOU COULD?

As we're travelling as a couple we're constantly balancing our time between work, adventure, exercise, shopping for healthy food and planning our next move. If I had my way I'd probably stay in bed in my PJ's all day online and then go out for sushi when it got dark but Luke makes sure that there's a time for everything.

WHERE AND IN WHAT ROLES ARE WOMEN IN THE LEADERSHIP STRUCTURE AT YOUR COMPANY?

I own my own company but Luke likes to think he's in charge. I've offered him a non-executive silent partner role!

HOW GOOD IS YOUR WORK LIFE BALANCE?

My work life balance is excellent, it's my freedom / guilt balance I'm working on.

BLOG - MAKING OUR WAY TO MACHU PICCHU

14th January 2018

Like most world travellers we wanted to visit Machu Picchu; the lost city of the Incas, unlike other travellers we are crap at forward planning so missed the chance to trek there via the Inca Trail – an ancient pathway which links all the major Inca sites high in the Andean mountains.

Machu Picchu is in the middle of nowhere, we took 2 flights, numerous buses & a train to complete the journey. From Lima, which is the nearest international airport, we flew to Cusco. Cusco to Urubamba was unexpectedly one of the most beautiful bus journeys of our lives! The snow-capped mountain landscape and traditional dress/hat combo of the local women was a lovely surprise.

After Urubamba, we went to Ollantaytambo for about £1 on the public bus. That's where you catch the Peru Rail to Aguas Caliente, which is at the bottom of the Machu Picchu mountain.

We'd already purchased our train tickets at a Peru Rail office in Cusco because with 1 million people visiting a year it gets busy. The cheapest train tickets we found were £65 each one way. The price for the locals is less than a tenner. You get a drink and a cookie though so that softens the blow to your bank balance a little.

We stupidly booked a really scenic journey for after the sun went down so both there and back was in complete darkness! No wonder they were the cheapest tickets! We went to Aguas Caliente around 7pm & stayed over so we could get up early and go to MP first thing. The train took 2 hours & it was raining when we arrived so we grabbed a room in the first hostel we saw. Luke wanted to look for another but I was tired so we ended up with a place with no Wifi, and no hot water or decent breakfast. The reason we didn't pre-book a hostel is that hardly anywhere in Latin or South America have an address system so it's easier to book somewhere on foot so you can be sure you can actually find it.

We decided to get the bus up to MP at 8am & walk back down the mountain later in the afternoon. I could see why they say the Inca trail is tough, just the walk from the ticket gate to the entrance was a challenge! There was another 9 days-worth of unthinkable pathways that linked all the ruin sites. Surrounding MP are loads of more ruins on the mountain tops, they wanted to be close to the gods so practicality went out of the window.

You have to show your passport to buy various tickets. If your boyfriend asks you to bring the passports and you don't, you may face, like me, an unnecessary 40 minute walk while your angry boyfriend ignores you and takes no responsibility for the fact he could have bought the passports himself. The ruins are over 560 years old & the workmanship is other worldly. It's like Stonehenge on acid, they have ceremonial sacrificial stones & researchers have found perfectly preserved mummies of children who were sacrificed. It's unimaginable but we witnessed the almost complete city of a mysterious lost civilization. There's evidence it was a spiritual retreat where the royal Incas experienced self-discovery through the plant medicine Ayahuasca which you can still drink in this country today. Our guide told us that the Incas built Machu Picchu in the shape of a Condor. Sitting above the site and looking down through the clouds at the ancient site was incredible.

PLANT MEDICINE

On a recommendation from Lucyne, a friend we made at Pachamama, we booked an Ayahuasca ceremony at La Pacha, Cusco. I was nervous, especially after reading and watching everything I could find on the effects of this psychotropic plant. One account by a Sunday Times journalist said the drug had him face down in the dirt of the Amazonian jungle facing his lifelong anger problem. On YouTube I watched a young girl speaking in a creepy child's voice with wide night-vision blank eyes. In 'The Last Shaman'; on Netflix the filmmaker searched for a cure for his lifelong depression, and a man died in the opening scenes. Despite this I felt like I was meant to do it! I was more than curious of what would happen and I saw it as a surrender. I worried for Luke as I had read that it's not advised if you've ever experienced psychosis, which he had in the past.

After getting a lift in a tuk-tuk down the longest road, flanked by high muddy brown mountains, we entered into a beautiful green mountainous area. La Pacha was a piece of gated land with little houses that looked like they were made of cookie dough, a cross between Gaudi's Guell park and Hobbiton. Pretty much exactly how you would imagine a village built by people on trippy plant medicine. There were beautiful birds around, the small community was creating utopia. Once we had taken a minute to breathe, we saw the amazing nature around us we felt at home. There was a big temple, built at the top of a hill, with views of strange beautiful lands stretching for miles. Other young European tourists began arriving out of nowhere and we all went to set up our stations in the big hall. We collected blankets, mats and sick buckets, the drug is known to make you 'purge', I really didn't want to be sick in front of a room of people. Behind us was a man, who wouldn't have looked out of place in the Twilight movies as a werewolf, and his girlfriend; slim blond, ethereal. We sat between them, and the host and his musician friend, who we saw emerge from one of the cookie houses earlier. The hosts made us feel at ease with their open, genuine smiles and slightly unkempt looks. One of them had been out of town and this was his first ceremony in a while. We sat waiting for the room to fill and had our money collected, we only had dollars which we hoped could be used here. After $60 each was taken we had an introduction to what might happen. It was new to us, aside from our all-night experience on Peyote. The host said he would call us up to drink one by one, play some music and then we could come up for 2nd or 3rd servings throughout the night. He said if we didn't know whether to come up then we should definitely come up! Luke went first out of the two of us. He is fearless, he wasn't concerned about the warnings regarding his mental health, at this stage I felt more concerned for myself than for Luke. I was really scared of what the drug would do and if I didn't react well, it would take 6 – 8 hours for the feeling to pass. Despite my well founded, evidence-based fears, I found myself up at the front drinking the foul tasting liquid. I took the vessel after it was 'blessed' with strong second hand tobacco smoke. That was it. I would know soon what 'Mother Ayahuasca' had in store for me. As soon as I sat back down, I started laughing. I had faced my fear, the medicine was inside me, there was nothing I could do but surrender. Luke and I settled in for the night. I began to see giant shadows moving around the room, I made myself a witness to the drug. I closed my eyes and saw green waves of energy from plants to animals and psychedelic flowing colours that reminded me of a poster I had seen in 'Athena' a hippy shop in Essex when I was younger; prisms, light. I enjoyed the live scenes. In the background I could hear a commotion, a large man was freaking out, being carried to the door, his skin screeching along the floor. Thankfully my trip was the green flowing psychedelics, witnessing and letting go. As the night progressed the music became hilarious to me. It was obvious the two men hadn't practised and were forgetting their cues. I could sense their playful, embarrassed energy as I had felt that as a singer in a band too. Luke and I found ourselves in a nest of blankets, crying and laughing, tickling each other, I felt like I was crying cold tears from my third eye as I had a flash of guilt on how I had left an ex-boyfriend after Nannie died. Guilt was coming up for me again and it was an obvious block to me moving forward with my life. Luke and I had never felt so close. I loved being there with him. Throughout I felt very sick, but I really didn't want to throw up. After 6 hours of hallucinations and emotions, the lights went on and everyone sort of came out of the trance. On closing the ceremony, the host said "you are not your body" that's all I heard before I had to run out to the loo, I threw up my lunch of kidney beans I had had 10 hours earlier. 'I wasn't my body', why was I holding on to the control over it? I let it all go, I purged everything and went back to my seat. It was over. We were allowed to stay in the hall overnight and at sunrise we packed our blankets away. We hitchhiked back into town, floating around a restaurant garden as we took our time ordering breakfast, feeling light, grounded, whole and cleansed to the soul.

ARGENTINA

January 16th 2018

Argentina is the steak capital of the world. Just great for two new vegans! I found a beautiful apartment on Airbnb where we would be staying with a lady in her later years. The whole flat looked gorgeous and was just £20 per night. The apartment was as lovely in real life as in the pictures. The Pantene shampoo in the bathroom reminded me again of Nannie. This small home comfort contrasted how 'out in the wilderness' we had been. I felt home. I looked in the mirror at my body for the first time since I could remember. My waist was a little slimmer. My hair was starting to look like a short crop rather than a microphone. I felt feminine and I couldn't wait to buy some new clothes having already spotted a boutique over the road. Each day I looked in the mirror there was a new reflection looking back. My hair was an ever changing reminder of the insecurity and freedom that came from starting anew.

As Alicia squeezed our fresh orange juice with breakfast each morning I was so glad I booked an 11 day stay. We took Alicia out to dinner and enjoyed some Argentinian Red while all getting to know one another. She had grown up children, one of whom lived off grid in the countryside while she lived alone.

My favourite childhood film was Evita. I used to watch it everyday after school. Evita is the story of Eva Peron the 'People's Princess' of Argentina. Eva made such an impact on the country that when she died in her early 40s the country sold out of flowers and the three neighbouring countries too. No round the world trip for me would be complete without a visit to her grave. Unfortunately, Luke had discovered something called 'free walking tours'. In my opinion all walking should be free but I was keen to learn about Argentina so we joined a walk that would end at the cemetery. As an introduction to the walk the lady guide spoke in length on how much these tours should cost and that perhaps we would consider donating at the end of the walk. This pissed me off straight away. Her voice continued to grate me for the next 2 to 3 hours by which time we had arrived at the cemetery completely exhausted (me) and more than ready for lunch (also me). I didn't have the energy or enthusiasm to look around the cemetery which is all I had wanted to do in Argentina. Luke and his boundless energy could keep going but I needed a rest and a new pair of eardrums. I needed to learn how to put my foot down. One old man had even passed out on the way round it was such a struggle. Dejected and on fire in the midday sun, we looked around a few tombs before I really needed to sit down. People were still queueing at Eva Peron's grave decades after her death.

Dragging Luke away from another walking tour that was just starting we found a gorgeous little café for lunch. Usually everything seemed better after a rest but that day I just really needed to sleep. We ended up walking 30 miles in 10 days thanks to 4 walking tours in total. There was a lot of beautiful architecture, history and statues to see. We saw the Falklands War Memorial for the 600 plus men aged 18 -21 who died fighting to reclaim the Falklands from the British in 1982. Many were in their first year of compulsory service. Six-hundred more committed suicide afterwards due to PTSD. Before this, Argentina hadn't seen war for over 100 years. The islands are called Islas Malvinas by the locals who are taught in school that the islands belong to Argentina and all maps made there show the land to be theirs.

NEW ZEALAND

I was able to give my malaise a name in New Zealand: home-sickness. We had been away from family and friends almost 7 months. The countryside looked like England as we passed the sheep filled fields. I recognised shops like Subway and the RSPCA. Familiar surroundings yet we were the furthest away from home we had ever been. Of course we were surrounded by English travellers but none were family, and I missed the friends we had left at home. The sickness crept up on me like a hangover I misjudged. I had overindulged in travel and I was feeling an unexpected side effect. To improve my mood I finally bought myself a travel sized guitar with a case and capo for less than £130. For months I had been writing in my journal that I needed singing and music in my life. Luke had concerns that a guitar would hold us up at airports, it would mean I would have to check my big bag and take the guitar as carry-on. This was the reason that I had delayed buying it for so long but practicalities had to give way to creativity, I needed this outlet. Luke treated himself to a harmonica and we were all set to be a travelling band.

Back when we booked our plane tickets in Nottingham, England, they had a deal on bus travel around the north and south islands of New Zealand. Unfortunately, we discovered once we joined the tour that STA's demographic is gap year students. Not a problem we thought at first, but after a week of late-night drinking and early mornings on the road we began to fray around the edges. At 31 I realised just how far in the past my student days were. Sharing smelly, noisy hostels wasn't for us. How do teenagers drink so much and still get up the next day?

We visited Hobbiton, the set created for the 'Lord of the Rings' film. We walked for an hour around the 'Shire' and visited a quaint tavern serving a traditional apple cider. We had photo opportunities in front of round doors, one of which Luke comically fell backwards through. I spent the whole time ambling around the hobbit village wearing a pair of novelty oversized ears.

Tour 'add ons' were announced each day such as skydives, bungee jumps and helicopter rides. At a bungee centre we listened to the history of the bungee jump and learnt that it was a 'coming of age' ritual of native African teenage boys, they would tie vines to their ankles and hurl themselves towards the ground from a makeshift platform high in the trees. Our history lesson came from a giant screen opposite a floor to ceiling windows, where, on the other side people were jumping off very high platforms over a torrential river. I watched closely as a woman was being guided to the edge, I expected her to dive off and for the camera to pan out to show the exhilarating journey to the bottom but I waited and she didn't jump. I realised it was a live feed. She was trying to overcome her fear of throwing herself off. The guy standing behind her did his best to talk her into it. I wondered how he'd fare if he encountered a suicidal person hanging off the Golden Gate Bridge. She turned round, and shuffled back, I knew that would be my experience if I ever found myself in her position. After Pachamama I vowed never to let fear hold me back but I didn't want to bungee. I worried about my eyes detaching, I hated being upside-down, I couldn't imagine ever being able to throw myself into the abyss, I wondered how I would feel after doing it, the buzz, would I believe I was invincible if I didn't die? Bottom line was I was going nowhere near finding out. Luke on the other hand had decided he would like to do it but was holding out for a longer drop.

Back on the bus after lunch, note to self, don't order a salad on a windy day and sit outside, the driver announced that Luke had bought a gift for his 'wife'. Random I thought, we're not married, and it better not be a bloody sky-dive, the option of a helicopter tour of a glacial lake might be nice! It was Valentine's day and Luke wanted to 'treat' me. As grateful as I am for presents, when the only things on sale are extreme sports activities that can kill you, it kind of dulls the shine. Anxiety kept pressing me to search for clues. Of course, he wouldn't tell me, and the driver kept making things up when I asked him. I breathed deep and decided to enjoy living in the bliss of ignorance for a few hours more as I knew Luke wouldn't be able to keep it a secret for long. The next day it all became clear, as we were picked up and taken to a small airport, my Valentine's gift was a Sky-Dive! My feelings ranged from panic, disbelief, denial, gratitude, apprehensiveness and wonder which circled round again and again.

Luke would be doing the jump too. I felt it was the better choice than a bungee, even as a gift I would have to have refused that. Although the jump out of the plane was at 14,000ft and the bungee just 43 meters, the parachute seemed safer to me than an elastic cord. Plus I would have Peter strapped to my back, with over 5000 jumps under his carabiner belt. If I was going to die, Peter was coming with me, and that felt reassuring. We had plenty of time to consider our fate as we waited all bloody day, for some reason everyone else went up before us.

New Zealand is an incredibly beautiful and diverse country, as we ascended, we saw the view of the Franz Josef Glacier. We hiked there the day before and caught a distant look at a solid blue waterfall. From above, the view was out of this world, a welcome distraction from the height we continued to gain. Just as I was beginning to see the curvature of the earth and wondering if the pilot was being serious, someone said: "half-way there". We were nauseatingly high, I was worried on the ground and now I was in pure disbelief. Was I actually going out of the door in a few minutes? Two guys had hitched a lift with us, it seemed they spent all day going up and coming back down when there was a spare spot in a plane. They were trying to get to 2000 jumps as that's the number they needed to become an instructor. Only Luke and I were left, this was it, as he was going out of the door, my stomach lurched as he disappeared sideways, securely strapped to his instructor, the way they whipped out made me worry about rotor blades, engines, what if we got caught in a propeller?

Peter and I shuffled to the edge of the cabin, the sound was all consuming, the roar of the wind and the plane's engine did its best to cut through my thoughts. I cleared my mind as best I could by looking into the white clouds, don't look down, be a banana, head up, legs up, hands holding on for my actual life. My feet dangled out of the plane, what if they got caught? Then, we were gone, into the clouds, the worst part was over, we were free falling and it was the best feeling I've ever had in my life, I embraced the fear, the unknown, the sky, and fourteen thousand feet with all my trust in a man I didn't know. I saw a tiny round rainbow in the clouds, free fell a little more and then the shoot was pulled. Floating back to earth was peaceful until Peter started to unclip where were joined together, I was being let go! It was horrible to feel like I was being dropped from a height, the same thing happened to Luke and we were only told afterwards that it's so we could lift our legs to land, a little heads up would have been nice. I was ecstatic after the jump and pretty sure I peed in my suit a little, but it turned out to be cloud water. Luke and I would have gone straight back up in the air if we could have, best Valentine's present ever!

Wanaka, New Zealand

We arrived at a beachside hostel, the atmosphere outside was like a summer barbeque, Luke and I made the most of it by playing UNO after dinner. A girl from our trip joined us and it was nice to have some company, if a little weird after being just us for so long. There was another couple, newlyweds around our age. We ended up in the same room as them a couple of times, and they snored really loudly! Luke wasn't having any of it and told them about how noisy they were the next day. Trying to keep the peace I asked them what their wedding song was, I promised I would learn it on guitar and play it for them on the beach. We arranged to meet them at the beach later but they left when we arrived, unsurprisingly. Luke has a knack of saying what is on his mind regardless of the consequences. Likely to do with his brain injury, it's important to him to have his opinions heard and his grievances aired. He doesn't have it in him to 'let it be' or 'grin and bear it' I admire this in him but at the same time it does make life more difficult than it needs to be sometimes. I'm maybe too much the other way and let things happen to me that I don't appreciate or enjoy but use them as life lessons. I have been called a pushover in the past whereas no-one is pushing Luke over in a hurry. We had a great time walking around the beach and visiting a tree that has been growing from the sea bed and has survived the ebb and flow of the Wanaka beach tide.

Amongst all the teens we met a man who was older than us on the bus. He revealed that he was taking the trip because his wife had died, his kids were meant to be here but he had ended up coming from England alone to fulfil a life-long dream. On the 1st February 2018 Luke had booked himself a bungee jump, in Taupo, New Zealand's only Clifftop jump. As it was his first he wasn't sure on the protocol and waited for the guy who had strapped him in to push him off. Once he was told he would have to do the jump himself he just went for it. I watched him dive down to touch the crystal clear water and then get picked up by boat! Impressive.

AUSTRALIA ROAD TRIP

Looking at our Melbourne host's bookcase I saw we had loads in common in terms of our reading tastes. When I asked her if she enjoyed the books she said that she hadn't read any of them! The woman wasn't overly friendly but we had a nice room. As we were now in Australia I was on the lookout for the giant spiders, especially as our window looked out to a webby side of the house. We would not be opening that for air. Luke spent a lot of time researching our onward journey as we would be leaving in a couple of days. I was interested in visiting the MOMA art gallery in Tasmania. Unfortunately Manic Mick had hold of the 'planning reins' and we were about to embark on a road trip up the whole of the East Coast of Oz. We both had an indiscriminate shitty feeling about it. We had found out from a couple in NZ that Europe would fit inside Australia. The East Coast is a solid 50 hour drive. We arrived in Melbourne on the 25th February and need to catch a flight from Cairns around 32 days later. Mick was adamant about sticking to our original plan and sadly I didn't shout loud enough about finding an alternative. We hired a 'Hippie Camper' which was a fraction of the size of the motorhome we hired in America and also didn't have a toilet.

My list of concerns included:

- Spiders.
- The heat.
- Violent Kangaroos.

- Sinking mud.
- Living in a small metal box for a month, with Luke, during the hottest month of the year.
- No air con in the sleeping area.
- No bathroom.

❋ ❋ ❋

Day 1 of 32 of our East Coast Australia adventures

(Must be read with an Australian accent.)

G'day mate!!

Picked the camper up and got ripped another new one! They love those last minute essential life or death add ons! What if you smash the windscreen..? A month is a long time to go without bursting a tyre... is it!? I have no idea. Here take all the money I have. Still, our Happy Hippie High Top rings in at less than what we paid for the 25ft tank we had on our U.S road trip. Once the bed is set up we share a half a metre square living space for teeth cleaning and late night Porridgo, (We've learnt that Aussies add an O on the end of most words.) We drove 4 hours today from central Melbourne to a national park on the coasto. Saw a giant kangaroo, a wombat, loads of medium sized Kangaroos, a crazy looking white bird with a giant thin black beak... maybe some kind of pelican... Pelo! After considering not going through with this trip we are now very happy we are here.

Day 2 of 32: L:

Today we planned to get up at 05:30am to be on the road to explore Wilson's promenade. After a later than planned night, this morning we kept "snoozing" the alarm and scraped ourselves up at just before 7... once on the road we had a walk around a wildlife hotspot on the prom and watched what we're convinced was a white faced bald eagle eating road-kill. Numerous groups of kangaroos and wallabies within touching distance and a few more foxes and wombats. The next plan was to trek Mount Bishop, but as it was cloudy and (Becca not fancying it) we went on a walk to cotters beach, where we saw more kangaroos and 2 giant Emu that looked like dinosaurs in the distance! I had been told on a trip advisor forum to drive 7/8hour days and have 2 or 3 days stop in places. After six hours in, and 2 hours short of the Bermagui location I'm aiming for, Becca has had enough, luckily I stumbled across a free campsite in Genoa. We then get out and jog (at Becca's request) to clear the air.

Additionally at Queen B's request, I then walked in the pitch black across a field to an old motel building, where I ended up knocking doors and windows pleading with them to sell me some wine to help calm Becca's shakes, the girl was stressed by the long drive bless her. I was grateful for the nice kale, lentil and falafel curry Becca made for my troubles.

Day 3 of 32: B:

Instead of the itinerary, I negotiate a day of free will and going with the flow. During this new democracy we met 'Old Tom' the skeleton of a Killer Whale in a fishing museum in a town called Eden. Old Tom; actually just 35, has been dead a while. Apparently he used to help the whaler's catch the big blue whales so he and his mates could eat the tongue. Today we attended our first folk festival too. We got quite tipsy and I managed to convince Luke that the pizza we ordered from an outdoor kitchen has Vegan cheese on - I'm sure he wanted to believe that as much as I did! The music was great but they have different rules here than the UK and you're not meant to take booze to the music tents.

Day 4 of 32: L:

We woke early from the Cobargo folk festival around 6.30am. We drove from our free campervan pitch (parked up on grass at the side of the road a 5 minute walk from the festival, free camping at its finest!) We've got no shower, so I drive back to the festival and I blag us back in for a wash. We head to Bermagui for a coastal walk along the beautiful beach. We meet a woman with a pet crow and see endless jellyfish tentacles spread every-where. After lunch we made our way to Jervis Bay and Hyams Beach, with pure white silky sand. But two beaches in a day is more than enough for me, so we go looking for accommodation and a meal out. We pole up at 6 different campsites to no joy all full. Instead we head to Nowra where we've been told will have some. Following a further knock back, I finally managed to book us into one 30 mins away. We see a sign and Becca convinces me to stop and we pull in. A fella in a white string vest looking like Charles Bronson comes out from a near-by caravan. Becca's tired, so we just pay for the night. At closer inspection it's hillbilly central and for anyone in Newark knowing seven hills, this makes it look like Beverly hills! We find a beautiful Thai restaurant 5 minutes walk away and eat there, despite not arriving at camp until 9pm. Shits "n" giggles as they say.

Day 5 of 32: B:

Today I drove us from coastal Australia, to Canberra, the capital and remember when I was too scared to drive the Lincolnshire bypass. Today was another good day, a lazy Sunday, just a 2.5 hour drive from the crazy campground of yesterday. Our $30 spot was next to a busy road but we were so tired from the long drive and long search for a campground that we still had one of the best nights' sleep. We filled the camper with a supply of fresh water and charged our phones. Luke is in his element now rationing gas and water as well as our food. Tonight we found a beautiful riverside campground with a modern toilet and shower block for free. It's near a hauntingly beautiful moun-tain top observatory which we drove up to tonight just in time for sunset. The old observatory burnt down and is now a great place for wildlife watching! We saw a fox chasing Kangaroos.

When we see a sign by the road saying watch out for wildlife we see animals every-time. It's rivalling Costa Rica and we've only been here a few days. We passed through a town full of cockatoos and have seen animals we can't even name. We are getting on well in the Hippie Camper...so far.

Luke worked out tonight while I finished the red wine and cooked pasta for tea. I listened to Dolly Parton & thought of my family who I love and miss especially approaching the anniversary of my Nannie's passing.

Day 6 of 32: L:

We arrived in Canberra wish, we hadn't bothered to be honest, why this is the capital is beyond us, an Aldi trip was our highlight! We go to one of the biggest buildings in Canberra- the Telstra tower. The views over the city are ok, but the interior has not been maintained and pretty depressing. Becca says Canberra reminds her of Scunthorpe. After leaving the tower we walked around black mountain, where we were promised to see 'magnificent views of the city' which really is not the case as the overgrown trees block everything. We'll be glad to see the back of Canberra. We are heading to Sydney this morning.

Day 8 of 32 - L:

Once in the city we have a tasty lunch in "The Garden" followed by walking the Sydney Harbour bridge. We went for a walk around the Sydney opera house, which my grandad Malc helped build when he and my Nan our Dawny lived there many moons back. After finding out that Eskimo Joe, an Indie rock n roll band from the 90s, were playing tonight, alongside the Sydney symphony orchestra we decided to get tickets.

Day 9 of 32 : L:

Yesterday we walked 28,000 steps around the city! Today we decided to head to the mountains. We travelled two and a half hours to reach the 'Blue Mountain National Park' so called because the eucalyptus oils, dust particles and water vapour creates an illusion of a blue haze. We trekked the Leura cascades, Gordon falls and Elysian rock, seeing some amazing sights including waterfalls, a disused tram track, plus a weird looking giant black parrot at Narrowneck plateau!

Day 11 of 32: L:

Last night was our last in Sydney and I met up with 2 lads from Newark for a few shandies, just a shame Ian had his first game of the season the next day and Reece had work, or it could have quite easily been an all nighter! Top lads and great to see some familiar faces. Becca and I headed for 'The Rocks' street market, which was pretty pricey compared to the street markets in South America.
We went to the 'Fortune of war' Sydney's oldest pub for drinks and listened to some live acoustic tunes by a decent Aussie bloke. Our Jordan Stafford from Newark came to meet us for a few shandies. We had food and a little bar crawl in the harbour. Next it was onto Shangrila, one of the tallest hotel/bars in Sydney for a peev and look at the views of the city. Then came the flip flop fiasco!

B:

We were worrying about getting in the Shangri-la hotel because of our traveller footwear. On the way up the steps of the hotel Luke tripped and broke his flop flop... or as they say here.. he blew a thong! I recommended the SanUK brand as I've had my flip flops for 7 years and they are really comfy... Luke's have lasted 7 months.

Day 12 of 32: B:

We left our RV park and spent the day at Bondi shopping in the markets and eating Sushi. By 4pm we got on the beach! A lovely beach but a little overcrowded.

Day 13 of 32: L:

A serious driving day. Early morning pit stop for a pic at the Newcastle sign, We have a paddle in the warm river and feed the fish. Then we drove from Port Macquarie to Coffs Harbour. Coffs has a beautiful beach, crystal clear waters and hardly anyone around; paradise. We walk around Mutton bird island, whale and dolphin spotting, yet we only manage a turtle and giant stingray. Then it's onto Byron bay. As I rest up, our Maureen is left in charge.. next thing the 3hr drive becomes closer to 4."Sat nav gone wrong" she claims.. "course it has Maureen".We swap drivers half way through as dangerous Brian takes back over proceedings soon after we pull onto a roadside with other campervans for our 2nd night free camping, thing is these vans are up for sale and we're just trying to blend in for a free night's sleep.

Day 14 of 32: L:

Following a short stop and beach walk in Byron bay, we make our way to the Gold Coast to meet my Karate Sensei from my childhood; Kancho Alan Bainbridge and his wife Annette. It's just over an hour drive and we check in at Broadwater caravan site $48 for the night. It rises to $76 in a few weeks when the commonwealth games begin so we were lucky. We're asked to arrive for "little kickers" at 6pm, then stay on for the adults class 7-9pm. It was a great evening and brought back some fond memories of being taught karate as a youngster. Thank you to everyone associated with the ASKA karate hobby club on the Gold Coast, that helped to make our night and re-union one to remember. A special thanks to Annette for our bag of goodies and to Kancho Al for his dodgy directions. Only joking you're a diamond my pal.

Day 15 of 32 - B:

Luke's been a champion boyfriend too since I've mostly been crying with PMT. Polly has arrived and she's not able to cope with life on the road. We were really happy to get to the RV park though and I wrote this on arrival....

"Oh the rapturous delight of feeling heat and water on my skin simultaneously.
This is the RV park of RV parks for £25 we have a bit of land to call our own for one night with a plug and water supply. It's like we're at the Ritz after spending two days literally sleeping on the roadside. This park on the Gold coast reminds me of the one we stayed at in Vegas. It has two swimming pools! We have stayed at the worst, most criminally insane parks, until now. They even have a full length mirror, I've comboed a top with a new charity shop 5 dollar dress and I'm winning, not even bothered if the top has a stain on. The stain is nothing."

It's clear I've lost the plot nearing half way up the coast of what must be the biggest country in the universe.

* * *

I was feeling like a homeless pile of crap with an aching body to the soul so I thought salt therapy would be good. I booked us in for a massage and time in the salt room. It was bliss... for me. Luke was not keen as the masseuse was a man. (I didn't know this before I just saw therapy and booked it) he's had some 'bad experiences' before, and in Turkey while in the sauna I could hear him shouting "don't touch my bum" is this normal?

Day 16 and 17 of 32: L:

I've been out of walking action for a couple of days after being in agony with a burst blister on my foot, so yesterday was a chilled day at the beach. Today we got back on the road putting the walking miles in and back to our preferred jungle walks in Springbrook National Park, a world heritage site. After calling at the fudge shop and 'Faebrook Fairy Farm' for a drink, we start our trek, visiting Wunburra lookout, followed by Purlingbrook falls and doing the rainforest circuit walk. We saw numerous waterfalls. Following tea, we wanted to watch the sunset at "the best of all lookouts." By the time we got to the lookout it was becoming dark and fog was setting in. Still we'd come this far and we weren't gonna give up until we got to the viewpoint. It was a 350m trek in a pitch black jungle into fogs-ville, where we couldn't even see the stars. On our way back we saw a girl on her own in the pitch black jungle looking for animals! She's more bottle than me let me tell ya!

Day 19 of 32: L:

By our half way point on day 16 we had done just short of 1900 miles in 6 days. Personally I love being up early and on the move seeing as much as we can in our time, this keeps me well. What keeps Becca well is moving at a much slower pace, her bed and getting her work done. So we compromise by being in charge of a day each in the van and we'll carry this on as we continue to travel. I can't find any day spas in Australia. Becca's not doing too well at the moment so I've researched and found a retreat. We just have to get there by 10am, it's in Brisbane while we're still in the Gold Coast but I figure we can get on the road early.

B: We are driving against the clock towards a 'retreat'. All I know about the retreat is that I need it more than anything else in the world. We get stuck on a ring road twice that makes me so frustrated and angry I just shut off my brain. I have passed being able to cope. This journey has been too long for me. We finally arrive, late and the group had already started. Luke and I have a fight and I run off in search of the loo for a much needed wee after yet another long drive. After apologising for being late and for arguing on arrival. We leave the van behind us for now and breathe a sigh of relief, this place is green and beautiful. Thank God we are here. I book a double session with a healer called Ann Marie. Ann-marie was an extremely gifted healer, who integrated spiritual healing, Kinesiology, and medical intuition. She tells me that we have the power and knowledge to be better than how we were in the past. We have the ability to wake up and be present. She suggests I'm struggling because I'm more sensitive now because I'm a Vegan, the same happened to her when she stopped eating meat. I think she's right. I care more about the planet, animals, the rainforests and sometimes it's overwhelming. She lifted some heavy weights from me that day. There were Kookaburras at the retreat. Beautiful wise looking birds that have chunky bodies and large eyes, they eat beef mince, it was all very strange. We are learning a lot about ourselves and each other and how best to continue our trip to ensure one doesn't throw oneself out of a moving vehicle.

CARMEL'S STORY

"I moved here in 1988 and I always felt that the land was special. We were lucky back in those days that we were able to choose this plot before the area was developed. We walked over hills, we couldn't drive – there were no roads. We were probably meant to be here. I grew up in the local area, went to a Catholic girls school then met Gary and got married young, the year that I turned 20. When I was 23 Matthew was born, Gary had grown up on a farm in Victoria so always had in mind to have a bit more land. Many people get into Naturopathy through their own experience. Matthew was allergic to cow's milk, dairy, but I was unaware and kept taking him to doctors and not really getting resolved. I didn't know about the allergy and he became allergic to penicillin so the antibiotics didn't work. It was through a friend who said to me why don't you take him to a chiropractor. The chiropractor did one adjustment and said now take him off dairy and you will see a changed child. Within 2 weeks his teacher contacted me and said Carmel, what have you done for Matthew because there are other children in the class who are similar to how he was. What's the change that you've implemented? Then I thought, there's more to this, there's more to diet and there's more to doing things in a more natural way.

Then my own health came into consideration. What I was doing for myself maybe I could do better, I could do more naturally. I went to a naturopath and started a journey there. I thought; "Well, you love this." I love herbs. I think the universe provides us with all the healing we need, through plants. I see food as medicine. I then went to college and studied, qualified as a naturopath.

Along the journey, I wanted to be independent even though I was married. In those days I worked with people with disabilities which humbled me in so many ways. I was so lucky compared to others. I made some great friends in that area too, when I look at the big picture it brought me to where I am now. I know you have choices and you have a say but I think the big picture is there as well. You are tested. When things aren't going so well I think it's a normal human feeling, to think well: 'maybe I shouldn't be here'. Maybe this isn't right, but then you overcome that because the next day things are better. I love this, this is what I'm meant to be doing. Should I retire, downsize and have some money? But then do what? The question comes to me then "do what? I like to travel and want to do things. Spirituality is everything, and it's the essence of who I am. I grew up as a Christian/Catholic, married in a catholic church, and brought my son up as Catholic. I have no regrets, it was beautiful, it gave me a background to growth. It gave me something to add on to. When I did start to seek out and think that there is more, I want to feel more, I want to feel the love more, I want to encompass all of it, not just what the catholic church is teaching. I started to seek out other avenues, I've looked at all forms of spirituality to the degree that I went to an ashram in India out of Bangalore. It gave me another insight. I've done many retreats with different groups and each and every one of them was just confirmation of 'this is who I am' in this lifetime. This is where you're meant to be, this is your journey. This is the love that you want to tap into, I suppose it sounds corny but there is this magnificent energy that's around us that I want to share with the world that there is something special there. It's not just this day to day experience."

* * *

L: Carmel offered us a free camp at her beautiful home on Saturday night and when Sunday came, she cooked a veggie roast lunch, shared wine, while washing our clothes for free and offering further free nights accommodation! We really couldn't thank her enough, she offered Becca work this Saturday at her next retreat doing Reiki and Social Media and me doing Yoga, exercise and numerology. She also offered to pay us and to stay free of charge. It was tempting, but time to move on. Our relaxing Sunday at Harmony place was spent taking in nature, getting work done and shopping for the week.

B: Very tempting!! My stressed eye twitch went crazy when she asked me to stay and do Reiki... My eyes were like DO IT!!! It would have been very relaxing and rewarding. I'm sure if I had been on my own I'd still be there now - still recovering.

Day 21 of 32: L:

Today we had a lie in (Becca's day) then I did yoga and an exercise circuit before we showered and got on the road. We did part of the coastal walk in Noosa National Park just short of 6 miles, we spent time sitting on cliff rocks at dolphin point overlooking the sea. In the afternoon we drove to Hervey Bay and early evening met up with Darren Marshall, who my friend Jonty put me onto. Darren is a top bloke and has offered to put us up while we're here, which is a bonus! We take some beers round and sit with him and his partner watching an episode of "Married at first sight." A rare bit of a programme to be honest! The last time we watched TV was the Canelo triple G fight last year. It's good to chat with someone who talks the Newark lingo... "Sound Chavi"

Day 22 of 32: B:

We went to look for Dolphins! Magically we found them. The camper is parked up and charging while we sleep in a comfy bed.

Day 23 of 32: L:

Today we went to Fraser Island. It's the world's largest sand island and a World heritage national park. We swam in Lake

McKenzie, with its white sands and clear turquoise water. In the afternoon we walked through the subtropical rainforest and saw 2 Dingos. We had an all you can eat vegan friendly buffet and paddled through Eli Creek, whose waters are considered to be one of the cleanest in the world. It was our last night with Darren & Sharna. We're grateful for everything Darren did for us during our stay. Sounded like an Aussie the first night I met him and 5mins in we're all on the mush n geera reminding me of home.. bless ya.

Day 24 of 32: B:

Yesterday we drove over 8 hours from Hervey Bay to near the Great Barrier Reef, I had a little cry but mostly it was ok. We passed through a town called GIN GIN where we got some of our country flag badges sewn on our backpacks and Luke treated us to some new hippy necklaces and some Frankincense to burn! It smells divine and has given the stuffy van a good cleansing.

Day 25 - 31: L:

Our 25th day on the road was spent in the camper at our caravan site for Becca to get ahead with work. We also had a torrential storm, which felt like a Cyclone! It rained all night and when we woke today it was still raining. We only have a few days at Airlie Beach to visit the Whitsundays and the Great Barrier Reef. As Becca's birthday was coming up I booked her a surprise yacht trip, with tours of Whitehaven beach (one of the best beaches in the world) snorkelling at the coral reef and food included. A couple of hours in and just as we were getting wetsuits for our first snorkel, the captain announces the engine has failed, so we've literally got to go with the wind the long way around numerous islands to try sail back to the harbour, then it started raining again. 5 hours later, no swimming, no snorkelling, no island tours. We were collected 10 minutes out from shore in a narrow boat. The luxury yacht tour wasn't exactly what we had in mind but I did see another dolphin. They only gave us a partial refund for our wasted day. Neither of us fancied sailing again tomorrow, so I'll book another tour to see the Great Barrier Reef when we get to Cairns. Light and dark of travel life for sure.

AUSTRALIA WAS ONE BIG LESSON TO LEARN - BLOG BECCA

"Everyone else is ok." the owner of the boat said to me as I complained about the broken down yacht. Apparently all the other people on the boat trip were fine about a partial refund. What should I be too? I'm not. And then I cried for the second time that day. I'm not ok because I'm hungry, I was sick on the 'boat trip' and when I felt better the host had thrown the food away. That was the first time I'd cried.

I'm not ok because my hormones are out of balance.

I'm not ok because my emotions clearly are too.

I'm not ok because I've been tired for as long as I can remember.

I'm not ok because I feel like shit for missing my Mum's 50th birthday party.

I'm not ok because now I care too much about things I never thought about before.

But… Everyone else is OK."

Day 27 of 32: B:

We've had a shit few days with day-long drives and being stuck in the van because of rain so we needed to chill. We got up for a bit of yoga in the morning but it went downhill from there (for Luke anyway). I went to do some work and was very happy to sit in a coffee shop with a nice lady bringing me water throughout the morning but Luke's clothes were still soaking with all the rain so he went to find a Laundry... using Google Maps rather than his eyes to find it. Google took him to an industrial estate which only did industrial laundry. He had a very long story when he got back anyway. We drove a few hours and restocked our Mother Hubbard's cupboards and found a great creek full of mosquitoes to free camp at. You only have to cross the creek twice to get to the loos! Rain, rain go away, it's like camping in the UK!

WHERE WERE THE NATIVE PEOPLE?

Natives who lived in Australia for 70,000 years before the British arrived, were now just a mention on a tourist information sign. Did they move away from the edges where the Europeans settled and now live in the middle? My naivety was to be my downfall. The driving almost killed me, the driving and the arguing over 'not wanting to drive' and Luke saying we 'had to drive because that was the plan' made me so unhappy. Also I wanted to find out as much as I could about what had happened to the native people but the more I was discovering the more depressed I was becoming. I bought a book called 'Sapiens' and tortuously I found out everything. I looked on Wikipedia to discover that 98% of the native people of Australia no longer exist. I found out that Tasmania, a small island was inhabited by a unique population who had been alone on the island for 10,000 years. Within 100 years of the British arriving there they were all dead. A whole civilisation wiped out, through diseases they had developed no immunity for and some through suicide as they were so against becoming westernised by the invaders. We took their children away because in our western eyes they were unfit parents. When they fought back, we imprisoned them. Luke asks me if I want to go on a tour of a prison. He thinks I'm in a mood for no reason. I think I've spiralled into despair because of the death of 98% of the population, too long drives and a boyfriend who doesn't listen to what I want.

* * *

I start to read 'The Power of Now' to balance myself. It teaches that there is no past, there is no future all we have is now. Eckhart Tolle, asks: "How is it possible that humans killed in excess of one hundred million fellow humans in the twentieth century alone? Humans inflicting pain of such magnitude on one another is beyond anything you can imagine." I can't get away from the facts of humans killing humans. I remember how I felt at the Holocaust memorial for the murdered Jews in Berlin. Sick. To. The. Stomach.

By changing books, I can't avoid this truth and I have the old saying in my mind of 'if you're not part of the solution you are part of the problem'. How can people overlook this? Why aren't we ashamed? Or are we channelling our shame into action, building more cities to distract ourselves?"

Day 28 of 31: L:

As we near the end of our trip, I've loved it. I know Becca has found it more of a challenge, particularly the pace we've done things at and she tells me she'd have just preferred to have got a plane to the centre of Australia and spent a month with Native Australians at Ayers rock. I'd still love to do that, but seeing the east coast by camper was a dream. Today we got up at our free camp at Alligator creek (didn't see any though.) I'm reading a lot about vegan intermittent fasting and am fasting at least 16hrs a day and have an 8 hour window to eat.

* * *

Australian Interlude

I had a Lonely Planet guide of 'East Coast Australia' on my shelf for many years at home. It was our dream to do this road trip but by this point in our journey we knew we preferred being in nature. So in my opinion, our plan to drive up the East Coast of Oz had become obsolete. There were good things about being on the road, the views, our bare feet, the 'Roos' and the fact I'd stopped wearing a bra. But the bad things made me want to throw myself out of the 'hippie camper' while it was moving to feel the sweet sensation of the road tearing off my skin. I don't know if it was boredom, cabin fever or the fact that we had to piss in a saucepan as we had no loo. Our fridge door would not stay closed so daily we had to retrieve all the fruit and veg from rolling around the camper floor. Luke had decided to start fasting so sometimes we had to wait hours for breakfast. I would fast too as I could see the benefits of Luke doing it and thought it would be good for me but my blood sugar would dip so low that I felt suicidal, fasting while on the longest car journey of my life was not a good combo.

I tried to get my work done by battling with Tesla; the Australian phone network to activate the 3G mobile data we bought in Melbourne. A guy had sold us 'the perfect solution of internet coverage on the go' but what we actually got was over an hour on the phone each week negotiating re-activations, because according to the head office the offer ended the day before we paid $80 for it. Mornings were spent hangry and guilt ridden about the shoddy work I felt I was offering my clients and anxious about the continuing availability of the internet. On day one of our road trip here we were amazed and excited to see Kangaroos for the first time, being so close to at least 30, just us and them, was incredible. Some were so tall we didn't know whether we should get any closer, the sun had completely gone down so walking the trail we intended was out of the question (at that point in our trip it was anyway –by the end we were walking around in the dark). It was a full moon, the stars were out, and strange beautiful animals surrounded us, looking back, that was one of the best nights we had in Oz and our year-long trip overall. We were full of wonder, apprehension (knowing this road trip would be eventful). I look back on that night and can still feel the flutter of excitement in my heart. The same feeling that I got when I quit my job, booked the tickets to leave the UK, started my own business, a massive fear of the unknown but embracing it, looking over its shoulder to see that everything I want is on the other side. Australia is really beautiful, I got to appreciate that when Manic Mick appeared one day and drove the van off without me. I sat barefoot by a lake just watching the ripples made by more unknown creatures beneath the surface. I watched a jellyfish the size of a dinner plate from the warm wooden decking. Luke came back and apologised. I took over the driving and we attempted not to fight again about the sat nav which had no idea where we were a lot of the time. Not helpful when navigating a whole giant country full of strange animals that would likely kill you given half a chance.

Day 28 of 32: L:

We're on the road again for a 4hr drive to Cairns. Cyclone Nora has been wreaking havoc with northern Queensland and in the last 4 days, apart from a few hours when we were on the yacht at sea, the rain has not stopped. We contacted the camper-van place about returning our camper to another location, but we're told the Cairns roads were open. Kancho Alan, had warned us that they may not be. Still the positive and determined pair we are, after checking different travel news, decided to try, only to be stopped 3 and a half hours short of Cairns at a roadblock. Bruce Highway to Cairns was closed due to metre high water on some parts of the motorway. The alternative route is also closed after a landslide. So we pay for power and a shower for the night at the nearby Crystal Creek caravan site. I'd booked us surprise tickets to a festival/concert in Cairns tomorrow evening, so I'm hoping the roads will open and we are somehow able to make it, time will tell.

Day 30 of 32 - L:

The poxy alarm never went off, but I woke at 05:30 and we were on the road before 6am. We continued our drive to Cairns and arrived at the botanical gardens just before 10am. I'm still keen to snorkel the Great Barrier Reef before we leave here, but as it's Becca's 32nd Birthday weekend as a thank you for her great determination to complete our road trip, I've treated her to 2 nights in a luxury tropical rainforest spa retreat.

My Birthday - Becca

All the things I love:

- Wine
- Limoncello
- Vegan cheese

- Relaxing
- Sleeping
- Breakfast in bed
- Second breakfast in the outdoor Hot Tub
- Kundalini Yoga in the private garden overlooking the rainforest.
- New clothes!

Very grateful for my lovely gorgeous boyfriend getting the memo that I need to relax occasionally, thanks for a lovely birthday. 32 today and travelling the world. I'm very happy and rested. Looking forward to a late check out tomorrow, returning the van and getting ready to catch our flight to Perth which will be our 8 month travelversary! Two nights at the Platypus retreat makes this whole drive here almost worth it! I bathed naked in the outdoor bubble filled hot tub, floated luxuriously in the pool while Luke did the majority of the cooking. We ate our meals in the bubble pool and the host who we didn't even have to meet in person had baked us some bread to enjoy with the marmalade that was in plentiful supply. The contrast between the dark days on the road to this pure light bliss was palpable. The van seemed tiny and very smelly compared to even the driveway of this retreat. I closed the gate behind me and we never had to spend one more night in it.

PERTH

1st April 2018

On a bucket list I had written in my mind, swimming with dolphins was at the top. I imagined it as a spiritual experience and was a little nervous to do it. We found a company called 'Wild Adventures' in Perth. Perth was a lot quieter and more relaxed than the East Coast and the slower pace suited me.

We were last to arrive at the boat trip, we caught three buses, likely we only needed one as I'm pretty sure that the second bus took us in the opposite direction. As we got near the marina, time was running out so we had to jump off and ook a last minute Uber! All this stress and effort could have been saved had we just booked an Uber from our Airbnb, but we were trying to be economical, a false economy I reasoned, but with Morris's thriftiness I don't think he valued 'saving us stress' as a good investment. He likes to be against the wire.

For 27 years the staff at 'wild encounters' have been developing a unique experience where one person acts as a focal point for the Dolphins and moves like they do, and the tour group watches the wild Dolphins swim right by! One Mummy Dolphin brought her baby close to the boat, their interaction to each other felt as familiar as my own mother walking me as a child to the shop at the end of our road. The dolphins seemed to want to be around us, they were curious. One show-off dolphin followed our boat as we sped away, it surfed the waves we were making and the whole boat oohed and ahhed at its incredible acrobatics. Every time it jumped out was just as exciting as the last. Mutual satisfaction between us. If only nature and people could get on so well all the time.

We enjoyed Perth as the vibe was a lot more chilled. I met a couple of native Australians at a Karaoke bar & we sang country music together, the lady I met loved Dolly Parton as much as me. We met up with a couple who were originally from Newark for a boozy lunch and a peruse and the Op-Shops (Charity shops). Trudy and Nathan were so much fun and Luke and I loved being in their company. Sadly the night ended in an argument as I wanted to smoke menthols outside with Trudy. Luke didn't like me smoking. Trudy and I decided it was worth the argument as we filled the street around us with smoke and laughter.

BALI

Bali was bliss. We carried each other around in the pool weightless and giggling, I felt creative, relaxed, it was really like a holiday. It's a shame it only lasted 12 days. I wanted to stay longer but Mick wanted to get going. Singapore was next which was horrible, we left there and went to Thailand very quickly. I missed Bali. I'd bought a map of the island and I longed to return to explore it all. We did a few day trips, Ram, a young new father was the taxi driver for our hotel/apartment, there weren't many guests, so we were able to have him drive us to the main sites for cheap. Ram was sweet and became our friend. He would wait in the car and was often asleep when we returned. Luke had us all on a tiring schedule of seeing everything we possibly could. I felt as exhausted as Ram looked, I wanted to see everything as much as I imagined Ram wanted/needed this job, but Luke had no off switch.

We needed to work on our definitions of 'being a tourist'. Luke likes to dart between the top 10 attractions on TripAdvisor with no thought to logistics leaving me more desperate for that alcoholic drink or dare I say a lunch break, than ever.

We struggled to find any balance. If left to his own devices, he would see the whole world 'just so he can say he's done it'. We visited a rice field, at first it seemed like a self-contained attraction which we initially paid to enter but it soon became a maze of rice paddies dotted with check points each asking for more money to pass. Occasionally there would be things to buy like hats made of leaves and snacks plus attractions such as a bamboo cane replica of the titanic. We met a farmer carrying a large rounded blade, Luke asked him for a photo, naturally the farmer wanted payment; with suggestions from me that Luke should avoid arguing we eventually continued. But where were we going? We seemed to be coming off the tourist track and into the unknown. Before entering, the site looked like a simple basin but we had no idea which of the many layered pathways were the best route out. I wanted to go back but Luke wanted to go 'all the way around'. 'I don't even know if you can, Luke'. "We can," he said. We trudged on, and on, in the boiling Balinese sunshine, and I could feel my skin burning, we asked for directions and people told us to go back the way we came. We went off in different directions for a while. Luke reached a dead end and had to come and find me. In the very end I dragged us through a stream in the general direction of the side we entered into. By the time we got to the roadside I was bright red, exhausted and in tears. I felt like my face was going to explode. "Why do we always have to push, push, push on? Why does every day need to be such a struggle and so exhausting?". Luke gave me some drinking water while I washed my trainers out at a tap. If I had known any of the people around me I'd have been embarrassed at the emotional and muddied state of me but thankfully on this trip there was plenty of time for my public breakdowns. Vegas was my favourite, in Bali I was the most red. Even Luke backed down from the resulting argument as he thought my face might burst.

* * *

You know the pictures of the swings you see over rainforests, usually on social media in a post aimed at getting you to quit your job and get on a plane there and then? We went to the place the pictures are taken! In the middle of nowhere, Ram dropped us at 'swing park', an area of Bali seemingly made for Instagrammers. Free coffee samples were supplied, for some reason Luke decided to upgrade and pay for a coffee that was made from the shit of an animal: Civet coffee. It was actually quite nice and sweet, the beans having gone through that unique process through a live animal's gut and anus. The experience continued around a selection of different wooden structures which swung terrifyingly high above the jungle. We watched for a bit while shoes were lost and attitudes towards getting that perfect pic changed as they looked down and refused to be pushed out above the jungle! $10 for three swings was a bit steep for us so we opted for a quick sit down in a giant fake bird nest, the ladder to get in was removed and our iPhones given to the man on the ground who could have easily taken off with them. I joked that the photos we had were our engagement shoot. I had wanted to get married in Bali since reading Eat Pray Love; the author falls in love in Bali and with Bali. Bali represented love for me, but we weren't yet engaged let alone in a position to get married. We were getting on better in Bali than in Australia though. Someone bringing us banana pancakes each morning was doing wonders for our love for each other. There were times during our trip when I knew that we were good for each other and times where I knew I never wanted to see him again. Morris moans a lot, when we are both hungry he finds fault with every restaurant we walk into and I'm exhausted by it. Just the day before our photoshoot we had to leave one eatery to go to another only for him to decide he's not going to eat, he's just going to sit there, moaning about the lack of service or the price of beer (about 20 pence) I was just beside myself with frustration. It's something we still need to work on, I understand that the moaning is just a symptom of his depression, an outlet for the pain he can't help, but fuck me, it's exhausting.

Luckily the food in most Balinese restaurants was absolutely amazing. We had discovered our first plant-based milkshake but Luke drank his and loads of mine and I'm still pissed off about that more than a year later. The city of Ubud was our base the whole time. We visited a silver and gold shop and workshop, basically, you get about 30 seconds to walk through a small room where 6 people are working on different items and then you're in a massive mall full of jewellery to buy. I spotted a ring just as some American lady proclaimed loudly "this is just a tourist trap, let's go" to her group. Well see you later moody Jane! I'm in and I'm sold. The ring was silver with a little gold accent on either side of an emerald green stone. I tried it on, and it fitted perfectly, the lady behind the counter was pushing the matching earrings but I said to Luke I'd love it as an engagement ring he had a look but didn't seem keen. We both left but he went back in 'to the loo' I thought he'd gone to buy the ring but he came back without a bag and said he had a bad stomach, he has had a bad stomach intermittently throughout the whole year so I believed him. There was no box, bag or telling lump of hidden jewels in his trousers.

The next night Luke said he had a surprise planned, it wasn't a problem but due to forgetting to do laundry we had only one clean pair of underwear between us. They were his so of course he got to wear them! All I had to wear (literally) was a thick, orange woollen dress I'd bought while drunk from an animal charity shop in Perth. It was a beautiful colour but absolutely boiling. I teamed that with a lovely long mala bead necklace I'd found at the market and a light wrap for my arms. Ram had been waiting for us and like a true gent, opened the car door for us too. He took us down the back streets that ran all over the city, hidden dark alleyways of beautiful stone and temples. A dog was really barking as we arrived at the reception area of a beautiful hotel. A lady led us away from the barking dog, thankfully as I was scared it would bite me. Although commando, I didn't have my dog beating stick with me.

The paths inside seemed to go on for miles, we were led past incredible carvings on traditional Balinese doorways behind which I'm sure were the most expensive and beautiful rooms on the island I carried my sandals so I could feel the smooth cool stone underfoot. We were led to a dining area with a swimming pool decorated with traditional flowers, we crossed the pool via bridge, passing a serving hatch from the kitchen, there were plenty of smiles from the staff who seemed super friendly. I noticed there were rose petals on the floor around our table and roses on the table too, there was a little table for my bag and as the restaurant was by the river, we were given bug spray! It was pitch black by this time, so the riverside table seemed a little wasted. Not deterred, we ordered some cocktails and began to settle ourselves into what became our most memorable meal together. In the back of my mind I was still thinking that he had bought that ring and somehow hidden it, that this meal was going to be our engagement meal and he was going to ask me to marry him. Although we don't believe in marriage, so I really wasn't sure what question was on the way if any. He had been very convincing of his tummy trouble back at the ring shop. We spoke a lot about our lives reminisced about our childhoods and how much we loved and missed our Nan's cooking. It was so romantic, candlelight, no-one around us. After our main course I noticed a man coming out with a tray, but he went past me, so I didn't think any more, then all of a sudden another man started filming us and Luke got down on one knee! My heart was pounding and all I could do was laugh nervously and remember to breathe so I could go with the flow. Luke did a lovely speech about our time away, our love for each other and asked me to be his 'Life-Lover'. I was so nervous I couldn't stop laughing! I said yes and he put the ring on my finger. It was perfect. The ring box was made of dried bamboo leaves all woven together. I loved that box, but it did start to grow mould pretty quickly, and I had to throw it away – I appreciated that it was biodegradable. I found out that after our trip to the ring shop, Ram had waited outside our apartment with the ring for ages, not sure what Luke wanted him to do with it, it was only that Luke went to order our banana pancakes ready for the following morning that he eventually felt ok to leave with the ring and pick us up the next day.

* * *

How disappointing to have left Bali. Nowhere on earth could compete with Bali in my heart. I was keen to stay on, forever, or at least until we visited a spa where we could lay in a milky rose petal bath carved from stone and get our hair plaited, or perhaps rent an apartment for a few years. Luke and I had an incredible time but Mick and Morris wanted to STICK TO PLAN. The plan we made on our sofa in Newark while our only guides were one book and the television.

SINGAPORE AND THE BADLY VENTILATED ANIMAL CREMATORIUM.

A David Attenborough programme showed 'the bay of islands" as a 'park' in Singapore which combined nature and buildings. We were keen to show our support to this utopia by sitting amongst the trees, picnicking with the butterflies and bees while humans and animals cohabited in harmony. Unfortunately, we were both too depressed to leave the AirBnB until night time, so a picnic was not an option on our first day in this new city. The tree/buildings turned out to be part of a music and light show, which was impressive (for a music and light show) but not the harmonious futuristic animal dwelling/city we saw on TV. Disappointed we had come all this way to discover a fake fantasy, we thought going inside one of the towers might change our perception of The Bay of Islands. $20 to go up to the top of the highest tree/tower, each? Ok, we're only here once and we did hear Mr Attenbourgh recommend it, didn't we? We got a wristband and entered a tired hallway which reminded me of the inside of an Alton Towers ride, stickers partly peeled off the walls. The cold metal staircase led to the top of the tower. On the rooftop bar there were really uncomfortable high seats, it seemed like they wanted a quick turnaround of people on this 'viewing platform'. Feeling a bit peckish we ordered some potato croquettes as everything else on the menu was meat. Vodka cocktails are vegetarian, so we had a couple of those too, the bill came to $26! We quickly noticed the heat had increased compared to being downstairs and it was a bit smokey. There was a really bad smell. Burning flesh. We realised we were over the kitchen and the tower didn't seem to have a good air con system. The bar was a hot smokey stench of smoked dead animals and not in a garden barbeque way, the air was so thick that we were enveloped in the smell. What we expected to be a futuristic vision of nature thriving in a commercial environment was a badly ventilated animal crematorium.

"We were having trouble with our accommodation in Singapore too. We couldn't find many hosts, Our place was not at the location described, we couldn't find the kitchen.

- The host was pictured as a woman & named Sue but from talking to him on the phone Sue is clearly a man.
- The 'quiet' location is on a main road.
- Sue is nowhere to be seen.

Our Uber driver tonight told us AirB&B is ILLEGAL in Singapore! No wonder it's been a bit dodgy.

We'd already asked for an early check out as it's so noisy and I was in tears because I couldn't find anywhere to store or cook food. The host gave us a refund for 3 out of 4 nights and then said we could stay tonight for free.
I was ready to leave Singapore after 2 nights. Luke had realised 72 hours after the fact that he should have listened to me when I said I wanted to stay in Bali. He missed Bali too. The rain and humidity and the concrete disappointment of Singapore was weighing heavy on his mental health. Depression Dan was in his element in our seemingly hopeless situation.

We flew out of Singapore without giving it any more chances. Cities were not for us. Something we knew but continued to forget time and time again."

THAILAND

April 26th 2018

Singapore was a distant memory as we approached the unmistakable rocky cliffs of Thailand and the azure blue waters. After a few hours below deck we made our way up to get a better look off the top level. We had both been to Thailand before but not together. It held good memories for both of us, I still longed for Bali, but Thailand would do! We flew from Singapore to Phuket overnight and as our boat reached our destination we were just waking up, this day was going to be a better day, in a better country for us. The 3rd country in a week!

After a little apprehension at the beer drinking 'youngsters' on the deck benches we sat down and got talking to a couple of lads, it turned out that one worked for an accountancy firm I used to manage the marketing for in Lincolnshire. They had a few months of travelling before going back to England to start new jobs. I felt like I didn't fit in with the crowd of travellers, wearing my walking boots instead of flip flops and carrying my big bag that I didn't trust leaving unattended. The guys were impressed that we were travelling for a year. People always were. I was impressed with their energy levels, their ability to drink beer on a moving boat. I was feeling weak. We were making our way to Ko Phi-Phi, Luke had described it as paradise, undiscovered. Unfortunately, in the 3 years since he discovered it, many more people had too. We passed coves full of Long-tail boats, with more around the outside jostling for a chance to enter. I felt the familiar injustice of humanity ruining things from seeing the impact of tourism on this island. 'The Beach' was filmed near here, but the cove was closed for the foreseeable future, the coral was damaged so much by boats and snorkelers that it needed a lifetime to recover, if it ever will. As we came into the white sandy beach and pier the Longtail boats decorated with colourful scarves were lined up on the beach, it was a beautiful scene, but very busy. We headed straight for the first bar on the beach, Pirate Bar and had a few cocktails while searching for a place to stay for a few days. I found myself buying a Union Jack towel, I loved it and laid on the beach the whole day, the sea was clear and warm. Thanks to the beach day we relaxed and vowed to stay away from cities for good.

As we walked back to our apartment, we saw a load of bamboo/bungalow structures that looked like the perfect place to live were it not for the 40 other bamboo bungalows surrounding it. They were lined up side by side and back to back making the site look like an open-air warehouse rather than a luxury beachside resort. The diggers and mass of construction debris would not make for a peaceful stay. There seemed to be no cap on the amount of buildings, boats and people. Away from the beach, Phi Phi has lovely lanes of shops, restaurants and bamboo tattoo artists. Apparently, it hurts more when they do it with bamboo rather than a needle. We watched some being done, they sort of knocked the ink in with a bamboo dart. At night the island sparkles with fairy lights and colourful lanterns, there was plenty of market stalls to while away the hours.

We planned to catch a boat tour at 12:30 the next day but as we arrived we discovered it actually left at 12. Some people asked us if we would join their trip as they had paid for someone to take 6 of them on a tour but two of their group were sick. They needed us to make up the numbers and make it cheaper for them, at first we thought it was a bit dodgy and that maybe they wanted to rob and kill us but we said yes anyway, it cost us about £13 for a half day tour. We bought some Bacardi Breezers, beer and crisps and were on our way. All day we toured the small coves and islands stopping in the middle of the ocean for sunset.

RAILAY TO TONSAI BEACH

1st May 2018

We were searching for something more secluded and Tonsai beach was calling us, to get there we had to wait for low tide and hike around the coast. It worried me a little doing it with my laptop but we precariously made our way there over rock pools. We forgot to pick up our laundry before we left so although our bags were lighter, we would have another hike the next day, back to where we came from! Tonsai was an interesting place with two halves of the beautiful island separated by a thick, grey concrete wall. The people who visit here are peaceful hippies so the wall was decorated with amazing pictures and quotes like:

"Only True Wisdom: Is knowing that you know nothing... so relax my friend and welcome to Tonsai"

"Use your anger to make changes"

"Love is the force that transforms and improves the soul of the world"

"Salford to Shangri-La"

"People often look for happiness like they look for their glasses when they have them on their nose."

"If not now then when?"

"Like all great travellers I've seen more than I remember and I remember more than I've seen"

As I was relaxing by the pool the next morning Luke came back with the washing, he found a shortcut inland and it turned out we didn't have to wade around the island at all. The features and benefits of Tonsai were becoming clear, one of the first quotes I saw was "enjoy the magic moments', I realised it was a place to do mushrooms. Also, food hygiene standards were at best negligent. Luke had been so adamant about eating at a place because they had wifi he rushed in and sat down before I could take a look at the menu, as I looked at the sign my stomach cramped up with a stabbing pain. I'm assuming that it was a premonition of things to come because the salad and veggie burger I ordered gave me the worst food poisoning of my life. Luke enjoyed a few days of sampling the local herbal and fungal delicacies while I had my head over the toilet, throwing up so violently it also came out through my nose. I had flashbacks of learning to swim and nearly drowning. Why did I order the salad, clearly washed in faecal matter with the burger fried in old oil full of rotten meat? I went from spewing to laying with the room spinning to sitting on the toilet longing to feel better. By day 2 I managed a dry cracker but not even water would stay down. I read all the books on my kindle including ones I had previously abandoned, now they were my only crutch. While reading I discovered a story about a Nepalese OSHO disciple who opened the first OSHO centre in Nepal: the book ended with an invite to OSHO Tapoban. I had heard about this place before and started to think my sickness was a sign we should go there. I enquired, the place was genuine, and they had a course starting at the time we were due to be in Nepal, even with the accommodation and robes we had to purchase the whole course was affordable.

We would be entering into a Neo Vipassana, the meditation that awakened the buddha. Full of crackers, electrolyte sachets and hope for an enlightened future I joined Luke at the bar for the first time. I daren't eat anything but I tried one magic mushroom, Luke had 3 – 4 bowls of them and said they did nothing but one shroom on a completely empty stomach had me imagining the Thai version of Johnny Depp walking around the bar on one leg and occasionally morphing into a wolf man. We played Connect 4 for a bit, I met 3 albino hedgehogs behind the bar and decided it was time to call it a night being unable to rationalise if the presence of these hedgehogs was normal. My sickness was on and off until we left the island. As we waited to be picked up for a boat trip I had to go to the loo, there was no choice but to pay a man working in a tiny restaurant to use their 'facilities' which was basically a squat toilet. As we got on the boat full of other tourists Luke announced that I had diarrhea and sickness, great, thanks Luke. Sick and now mortified. Thankfully though, this prompted a lovely Australian girl to hand me what was left of her Imodium. I hadn't thought of buying medication! She said I could take three so I did, she assured me that the salt water would help to heal me too. I chose to believe her and a bit later I was one of the first off the boat and into the water. The salt really was healing and Imodium was my new best friend. We visited national parks teeming with stunning fish and used the GoPro underwater camera while feeding the fish fresh coconut flesh, it was brilliant. At one point I watched a monkey steal a girl's phone which was the cherry on top of bringing me back to life. Snorkeling under the water was peaceful, being on the boat under the sun was restorative. We got on so well when there were other people around. After this long trip together I felt that I should know more about how to get along better and I think I do: be around friends, don't drink too much or be around him when he's smoking weed, get sleep, eat when you're hungry and don't take the other person's moods as an insult. We would run into rough patches but the good always outweighed the bad. I think when the bad outweighs the good it's time to call it a day, but we never thought seriously about ending it. Personally, I felt we were growing together, every argument would bring a spark of knowledge about how to prevent the next issue.

Love ironically, has no limit to the pain it can cause but here's what I had learnt by that point:

- Ø It takes a village to have a relationship.
- Ø Sometimes when you think the world is ending you are just hangry.
- Ø Don't walk 3 miles for the big food shop after a day of wine tasting.
- Ø Stay somewhere at least 4 days before packing up and moving on, it's too much effort to move every day – unless you find yourself in Singapore, in which case leave immediately.
- Ø Plan some time apart.
- Ø Don't plan 5 things in one night with no phone signal.
- Ø Arguing in front of a casino full of people you don't know is liberating.
- Ø Don't eat salad at Tonsai beach unless you want to drop two dress sizes in a week.
- Ø Never trust a fart in Guatemala.
- Ø You can't prepare for learning the history of the atrocities of humanity.
- Ø Visit a national park where-ever you go.
- Ø The climb up to viewpoints is always worth it – apart from when there are armed bandits waiting for you.
- Ø Sometimes you are so thirsty that you will face down a man with a machete.
- Ø Your ancestors are guiding you.
- Ø The universe wants you to achieve your dreams.

It was almost time for us to leave that part of Thailand but we had to get across the country on a national holiday so transport was limited. Thankfully the girl who ran the tour that day called her manager and he drove us to the bus station, not before treating us to a fried coconut pancake and sugar treat, which was absolutely amazing. The kindness of strangers in our many hours of need was heartwarming and really changed how a day was going. We got our tickets for the bus the next day and had a little wander around to find a bed for the night. I thought about the girl on the boat, her English was brilliant and she was clearly an intelligent, successful tour guide who had looked after a load of tourists really well all day. She confided that her partner didn't like her doing this kind of work, he preferred her to be covered up at all times with long sleeves and a hat. We were told that Thai people aspire to work in offices because being out in the sun all day, getting darker skin, is not aspirational as working on the fields is a poor man's job. Here all the Brits are trying hard to go brown and the Thais want to be pale. At this point, after a day in the sun, we were lobster red. Time for a cold shower.

BLOG: HOW TO SURVIVE A THAILAND SLEEPER TRAIN

As I wash my hands, after using the world's most foul-smelling toilet, I feel water splash out at my feet, the sink doesn't seem to be plumbed in. I dread to think what the wet was on the floor near the toilet. I don't understand why it smells so bad as the toilet is just a very large hole to the tracks. I realise people have weed on the floor. A single use of a Thai train toilet recalled my memory of Glastonbury's cesspit toilets in a flash. I imagine you should never let the bottom of your trouser legs, scarf or towel drop to the floor, if you manage to drop all three like I did you may regret not flying to your destination. I chose between the western style over and Asian 'squat' toilet'. There's a big open window in the loo so 'going' while stationary was interesting as I made eye contact with people out the window. Maybe the squat toilet would have been the better option! Although just two days ago I attempted the use of one while on the sleeper train to Bangkok and found it tricky to manage the movement of the train, my balance and the fact that I had food poisoning for over a week. The train had appealed because it was £220 cheaper than flying. The first leg of our journey from Hat Yai to

Bangkok was really enjoyable but Bangkok to Chaing Mai was a disappointing tale. Which leads me on to the subject of dinner. Luke and I were running a little late to the train station, we had time to get a corn-on-the-cob-on-a-stick but no proper tea so I said I would buy dinner on the train. Big mistake. Our tofu was so dry it looked like chicken so thinking it actually was chicken we attempted to send it back. They assured us it was vegetarian and gave us two banana muffins and small orange juices for free for reassurance.

Luke used the communal plug sockets but was a little worried that his electronics would be stolen. He kept a constant eye on everyone who came near... it turned out they were using the spare USB sockets on our fancy plug. As I settled down for the night I remembered how I woke just two mornings before in my sleepy confusion I waited for the noise and the shaking from my dream-world to stop. It doesn't stop, how anyone gets to sleep is a mystery but maybe the movement of the train rocks you to sleep like a baby. My beach-towel-turban I created to muffle the sound turns out to be way too hot 3 seconds later so I try to get to sleep with the noise. I forgot I was allergic to my ear-buds and woke up with burning lugs. The toilet closest to us had its door jammed shut. I spent some time standing between two carriages which is scary enough in the UK but here the tracks seem to switch and change loudly every 10 seconds. A trip to the toilet feels like an Indiana Jones or James Bond opening credits when you're not sure he'll make it out alive. The toilet I found at the other end actually made me retch which leaves me able to share with you that a unicorn sleep mask doubles as a cover for your nose. I had a new appreciation of people who walk around in surgical masks. Some bleach and a complete renovation of the toilets wouldn't have gone amiss. I'm worried Luke will wake up and see the Indiana/Bond stuck door as some kind of challenge. When I ordered the rank tofu meal, and cold water soup, I ordered breakfast too. The con-artist/waitress asked if we wanted orange with our breakfast, of course we said yes. Turns out these were EXTRA orange juices as we were to get orange anyway. Two small buckets of orange sugar liquid were delivered to my curtained off area at 5:27am and breakfast a little while later.

The experience of coming from a big city into a beautiful green jungle was almost worth all the other crap. We step off the train in the centre of Chiang Mai. The thought of security, passport control and queuing, only to then repeat the same process the other side (for around the 20th time in the last 9 months) makes me more of a train fan (Although the flight would have only taken 1 hour instead of 16!) I was still interested in travelling more of the world by train but I would be checking the quality of the train beforehand. Some are good, some are bad. I guess it's the luck of the draw if it's a last minute booking with no research. In a few weeks we'll be in India. Their 'palace on wheels' looks much more up my street but tickets start at $1800 each... how much is that in pounds? Probably more than the £20 each we spent on the Thai sleeper train!

Chiang Mai, Thailand, 16 May 2018 - B:

"The place we are staying at with Luke's school friend David 'Eddy' Edwards is a luxurious apartment in beautiful Chiang Mai in the North of Thailand. For the first time since Australia we've done a big shop. We have 2000 baht worth of organic vege so we are really happy. Naturally we've just been out for dinner. Looking forward to seeing more of Chiang Mai for the next 5 days before we leave for Hanoi."

20 May 2018 · Chiang Mai, Thailand - L:

"A power day with our uncle Eddy... We drove to the top of Doi Pui stopping off at a cafe on the way to take in the spectacular views, while sampling some homegrown teas. Next we drove to the hilltop tribe of Hmong and visited the museum there, which showed us different native tribes and their traditional way of life. On the way

down we visited Doi Suthep, the highest temple in Chiang mai, had a blessing from a monk and a reading from some fortune sticks. We also stopped off at Wang Bua Ban waterfall for a dip in the pool to cool off and watch the young locals jumping from trees into the water. Rounding off the day with an all you can eat salad buffet at sizzlers and our first 4D cinema experience watching avengers while the seats throw you about like you're on the waltzer! Loved it, he's a top lad our Eddy and we're very grateful."

23 May 2018: L:

"For our last full day in Chiangmai we visited the Royal park gardens in the morning. It was hot and Becca decided too hot for her to want to come to the elephant sanctuary I had booked us into, so I went alone while she had a pamper day. This was one of my best days of our travels. I met Dang and Lisa from California and chatted with them on our 2 hour drive to the mountains. This sanctuary came third on trip advisor of 258 things to do in Chiangmai and appealed as they don't ride the elephants or use hooks to discipline them and they are free to roam in the wild.We have a small group of 4 people and there are 5 elephants, so a real intimate experience. We're taken to meet the elephants at an enclosure where they come to cool off, Valentine the baby of 3 months is just too cute! Afterwards we pre-pare food for them by grinding rice and fruit together and moulding into balls with our hands. We then go to feed them, the big male daddy Dharma eats sugar cane and reminds me of his strength as he snatches a picnic basket out of my hands! The big females also enjoy the sugar cane, while the youngsters eat bananas. We walk with them into the mountains where they go to graze, chill and feed themselves again, as we all watch on in amazement, before walking with them to a nearby stream. At the stream we are given buckets and brushes to throw water over them and brush their dead skin off. They love it and we do too. An experience I'll never forget."

DAVE EDDY
EDWARD'S STORY

"I come from a small town and Chiang Mai has a small-town feel. The way of life here suits me. I'm studying for a BA in TESOL (teaching English as a second language). I work in a school but I find online work is far easier and pays double. Unfortunately, Thailand doesn't promote longevity in teaching positions. It's almost set up for people passing through. Financially, I won't see a lot of difference when I complete this course. It's for job security. It will get me in a school with better benefits. It is also a stepping stone to my masters in education, which will get me into a good international school. A master degree is really a minimum requirement for a well-paid position in Thailand. You need a work permit to work in Thailand. To have one you need to work for a Thai company/school that's why I can't just do the online work – digital nomad style. Without a work permit all work is technically illegal. Even replying to work emails while you are on holiday here! The visa rules are outdated and online work is not mentioned so it's all a grey area.

Outside my estate are typical Thai roads. Lawless, no one cares, or knows about the laws of the road. It's sad to say but death on the roads here becomes normal. A friend, neighbor, and work colleague of around 3 years, a good guy, was killed. He was in his mid 20's, had a one-year old daughter and he spoke Thai, just a typical British lad from London. The Thai paramedics have their own Facebook group where they post pictures of accidents and go live at the scene, there's no discretion, you see brains all over the pavement. On TV too there's no standards. I saw pictures of my friend on the road where he died. I saw the police on the corner, I knew there had been an accident, I was on a chat group with the other teachers at the school where we both worked. I'd only seen him earlier that day. I saw the aftermath of the accident on the way home from the gym as it was outside our house but I didn't know it was him as the paramedics had covered him and the bike. Our boss told us all about 4 hours later. A tipper lorry had turned into a building site and hit him then ran over his head, he was killed instantly. Sad, but as horrible as it sounds it is just a part of life here. Everyone knows someone that has died or been seriously hurt on the roads here. The main problem with foreigners is that they see how bad the Thais drive, then they forget everything they know and drive the same. Thailand is an easy country to live in and the people are great but the lack of organization is annoying. Nothing is ever done about anything. Problems are just left (check the news about Chiang Mai's pollution). But I suppose England has far more negatives than here. Yes, it's clean and organized but we pay so much to live there it's crazy. England is a grind. If you have time then you have no money, if you have money, then you have no time as you are always working."

VIETNAM

**When we say 'yeah' Vietnamese people hear
'chicken'. How weird must we seem?**

22 May 2018

We had 15 days in Vietnam and we wanted to hike, eat, cave and
visit UNESCO & world heritage sites. We sampled our first 'Pho'-
noodle soup for less than £1 and it was glorious. Our AirBnB was
just £11 a night. I wanted to visit Vietnam since I saw that Top-
Gear special on TV, I imagined remote, makeshift eateries in ex-
pansive leafy green pastures. The reality on arrival was a little
different. We got to Hanoi, to the sight and sound of one million
mopeds, and the dark smoky city was strange and beautiful but
not green. I had heard about a specialty; Bia Hoi. A fresh beer
that's brewed in the city daily and available from 18p a glass
which I was eager to try. We booked a food tour on the internet
and a young student came to meet us outside our little apartment. A food tour in Vietnam, with a local, in a city famed for
extremely cheap fresh beer, what could go wrong?

A lot. Our guide was a really nice chap, but he took us to try
deep-fried doughnuts from a greasy noodle shack, they were
sugarless and tasteless. Oh well we thought, a bad start but
maybe that is their delicacy here! Next stop a little restaurant
with no air-con where we sweated through a bowl of bland soup
with some carrot shavings. Thankfully we left there for the
open air, we noticed lots of little stools available to sit on, by
the side of buildings, we assumed they were the overspill of a

restaurant. We sat on 3 blue seats, all the blue ones were available while the red ones were taken. We were to learn that we should have waited for the reds! The blue stool owners, seemingly a gang of criminals, served us three drinks and three bowls of cold chips for about £30. We never saw a menu so couldn't argue the prices. We just assumed that everyone around us was enjoying themselves and so would we. They were the red stool guys, a completely different experience. Luke argued a bit with the tour guide who we had expected would know where to take us on a food tour seeing as this is what we were due to pay him for. He couldn't apoligise enough and footed his 3rd of the bill, poor guy. The food didn't get much better in Hanoi but perhaps all their specialities lie in beef or chicken, the best dish we had there was from a chain restaurant at the airport! In England you don't expect much from airport food. Aside from dodgy restaurants and mopeds, the streets of Hanoi showcased some of the world's best greetings cards, of finely created pop up boats with moving parts, and Ferris wheels with hanging cages, small square pieces of intricate art for around £1.10. They were impressive and beautiful, I bought just two, thinking that they would be available throughout Vietnam, but it turned out I was lucky to get those. They were few and far between outside of the city and much more expensive. Once back in England I saw a girl selling them for £10 each at Covent Garden market! We often saw business opportunities on our travels and made a little money selling bags in Bali but it was a lot of faffing around.

L: "After a few days in Hanoi, we decided to book a 2 day mini cruise around Lan ha bay, Cat Ba Island and Halong Bay. We were picked up from our Airbnb place early yesterday morning and driven to Han Phong city via Gia Luan National Park to board our 5* ferry the Unicharm. The staff were kind and friendly and we were treated like a king and queen. I'd already blagged a room upgrade with a terrace for less money and we were not disappointed! They went out of the way to provide us amazing vegan options and a 7 course lunch and evening buffet dinner, while also giving us a cooking class on how to *make vegan spring rolls. We sailed through the world heritage site of Halong Bay and past Tuan Chan island, Cap Bai Islet, Ngon Tay and Til top island. Our ferry had just 2 other couples on board and there were more staff than guests. I did a 3 hour kayak, snorkel and swim in between while Becca chilled on the ferry. Today we went on a bike ride around the town of Viet Hai and Cat Ba National Park, visiting local homes in the 300 person village."*

✻ ✻ ✻

After our luxury boat trip we had one last night in Hanoi, we got an hour-long tour of the old quarter; on a rickshaw. Which is basically a pushbike with a double seat on the back. Possibly the most dangerous thing we've done bearing in mind the traffic!! We planned the whole of our Vietnam trip on the plane journey there, we somehow got hold of a lonely planet guide and used it to look at the top 10 things to do. We then whittled it down to the top 3 – 5 things, which fitted in with the limited time we had in the country. We picked Sapa, a mountainous, remote area that borders China, where we could trek and do homestays with native rice farmers, a national park where we could see the world's longest cave and a trip on a boat to the Halong Bay. Loosely we did all of these things, but all was not as it seemed in the guide book. The 'Home Stays' turned out to be freezing cold 'shed shacks' where the family don't actually live and the national park with the longest cave requires booking a year in advance.

In Sapa (which borders China) we saw some horrific animal abuse. We arrived early in the morning after travelling on a really new and clean sleeper bus. We walked through a market where I saw a severed dog's head amongst the meat cuts. I ran outside and waited by a motorbike only to see it start to twitch. I realised there was a giant live black pig bound up like a torture victim on the end of the bike. We saw another pig in the same situation later on. Poor pig squealing out of fear for its life. We realise in England they are also transported to the abattoir but it's really open in Sapa and it was hard to see, not just because we don't eat meat but because it's hard to imagine eating a pet dog or driving your moped with a terrified giant boar sharing the seat. Aside from the animals on the menu and a crazed mountain woman grabbing me... (no idea why) we liked Sapa and were looking forward to hiking.

27th May, Lào Cai, Vietnam: L:

"We had torrential rain this morning in the Sapa mountains. We brave it and go on a day tour with May, a local woman we met at the bus station. As we trek up over the rice terraces we are joined by 5 more girls/women trying to sell us all sorts. The group dwindles down to two; Meme and Xai and they are like Becca's little helpers holding her hand up and down the muddy mountain slopes. It rained on and off all day as we're taken to the bamboo forest, a waterfall, four villages with people from different tribes , the Black Hmong, Red Dzao, Tay & Giày. We finished at the stone carving museum. Our Black Hmong guide May also offered us marijuana to end the tour, saying the police were fine here it's ok to smoke, "just be careful with the opium".

Facebook post: B:

"May had some very sad stories. They only got a hospital here in the late nineties and lots of women and babies were dying in childbirth, fortunately since the hospital has been built she said no more women and babies have died this way. Sadly though her own daughter and son died and two of her sons are disabled. She has one son who is married with children so she now has grandchildren too. I'm glad we were able to spend the day feeling humbled by this beautiful soul and the difficult journey round the mountain paths. May showed us a bridge where historically, unmarried pregnant mothers would be thrown to their deaths, because the family couldn't afford to support

the unborn child. We now have lots more gifts for you back home as that's how they make their money. We also overpaid a little for our tour and May was so grateful. I hope she's ok."

4th June 2018: B:

"Been feeling anxious all day. The roads are dangerous from Hoi An to Dalat. We google the Sleeper Bus company we've booked the journey with and they are very poorly rated. It's pissing down with rain. Monsoon kind of rain that soaks us while we look for the travel agent. It's not where Google Maps says it will be. The reviews are preparing me for the worst. No toilets on board, (it's a 13-hour journey), not enough beds, random people getting on the bus at all hours in the night. No toilet breaks. The office once we find it does nothing to put my mind at ease, the minibus that takes us to the bus stop is overcrowded. The air con doesn't work so the windows are steamy, the driver can't see out and he's on his phone, mostly not touching the steering wheel. The bus stop is just a roof over a dusty mud ground, the big bus is 30 minutes late and a guy shuts the door in my face as I try to board. He takes my big bag, but the storage of the bus is full of mopeds. Just like the reviews said. We rushed this booking after seeing the flights were £128 this bus ticket was about £20. I'm wishing we spent the money and flew but we're always spending money! I read more stuff on Trip advisor about the company and found a link to a bus crash from 2013. Bodies everywhere. Were they wearing their seatbelts though?! Literally, I have not felt as anxious about something since meeting hat rabid dog.

* * *

I never thought I'd get off the bus, I thought we would be at the bottom of a ravine, dead. I was pretty confident of this. So, when we hopped off the bus into the daylight of Dalat, we felt pretty happy to be alive. That ended for me as I attempted to find a usable toilet. The streets were really busy, we found an open air café with a passage down the back which I followed to the 'loo' I found a dark brick built structure off the kitchen which it seemed doubled as a playroom for a little girl in a Disney dress, the toilet bowl was covered with a wooden board and there was no door to the space which barely contained the brown stained toilet. I learnt that you can be so desperate but still have the ability to hold on for something better! Talking of toilet humour; Luke struggled to use the 'bum gun' (hose) in the toilet on the bus last night. It worked fine for me but after doing a number two Luke got quite upset and shouted to the driver that the hose wasn't working and questioned 'How am I meant to wipe my arse?' loudly in front of a crowded bus full of people. I was absolutely mortified.

CAMBODIA

Luke and I had argued about keeping Cambodia and Laos in the 'South East Asia' part of our journey as well as Thailand and Vietnam. We only had a limited time because we had our flight booked to go to India. In my opinion we needed to drop at least one country from our itinerary to avoid rushing around and not making the most of the country we were in. He wasn't listening to me, he wanted to plough on through every country we had written down. I felt very frustrated and unheard, I was tired. We wrote on our Facebook group about our 'first world problem' of having too many countries and not enough time, I thought that Luke would see reason if more people made suggestions to do less. Most people said just stick to two countries, but Luke only chose to take notice of the ones that supported his argument.

When he was really ill, being sectioned and was taken to various mental health institutions, he had a care team consisting of his Dad, Dawny & his Auntie Caren. In saner hours he would seek advice from his Aunt & Dawny, when manic he would try to get support on his grandiose ideas of escape from his Dad. When no-one supported his plans he would do his own thing despite all his family being desperate for him to take their advice. Here I was his only constant companion and I worried that if he got ill, I was the sole member of his care team. How could I care for him when he didn't listen to what I saw as reason? Mostly I was rail-roaded into doing things I didn't want to do. Like the whole of Australia in a small hot van. Somehow this time, we compromised on leaving out Laos. My negotiation skills after 10 years in sales had come to good use. After 10 months of travelling I was winning arguments about cutting out countries we would see, ironic for someone who had wanted to see the world.

Cambodia was busy, dark and smelly, it seemed to be much poorer than Thailand or Vietnam. Although there were no roads or paths, just dirt tracks and dust, the food and drink was sublime. We found a restaurant with the best rum cocktails of our trip and a 10 hour marinated Tofu dish. We had 5 days to see all the sights. 'All the sights' turned out to be mass graves along-side schools which were converted into prisons and torture chambers used up until the mid 70's. Thankfully Cambodia also has the biggest and most beautiful temples in the world. Angkor Wat was on our list as well as the temple used in Tomb Raider. We visited a school called S-21 where innocent Cambodians were imprisoned and tortured by the barbaric Khmer Rouge. Cambodia had a chilling history, so we prepared ourselves to some extent. Personally my preparation was a feeling of total dread and anxiety before walking through the gates. I had been to Berlin, sadly hungover and not really expecting to see what I saw. I didn't realise before that day how appaling the holocaust had been, that was a big lesson in European history. I came out of there questioning everything I thought I knew about com-passion and humanity. Any amount of research couldn't have prepared us for discovering the history of Cambodia, where three million Cambodians were murdered at the hands of their own people. I was heartbroken and in tears to read some of the first-hand accounts of 12,000 - 20,000 Cambodians killed at that prison. We spoke to one of only 5 survivors of 'S-21 Prison' which is now named the Tuol Sleng Museum of Genocide. Chum Mey, a kind faced old man, came back to the prison daily to tell his story and sell his book on how he was tortured by the Khmer Rouge. I asked him, through a translator why he came back; he said he 'had to tell his story'. I bought his book, it was the least we could do, I stood by his side for a photo and told me in about 3 English words and horrifying gestures how they had electro-cuted him through the ear and pulled out his toenails in order to get a fake 'confession' that he was a spy. The photos of me with Chem Mey show me with tears in my eyes. We read about a man from Newcastle, England who was killed in the genocide, he had been travelling with a friend from New Zealand. Like the Cambodians, he was shackled to the floor, kept confined night and day, and was forced to 'confess' to being a spy. Many of the written 'confessions' were there for us to see. John Dewhurst told his captors his father and himself were CIA spies, that his Dad used his role as 'Headmaster of Benton Road Secondary school' as cover, and that he had learnt how to be a spy in Loughbough. John's confession at 26 years old made me think of how ludicrous it had been for Pol Pots and his regime to assume everyone was a spy, when in reality, John was a travelling yachtsman and the Cambodians were some of the most kind, quiet and gentle people you could meet in the world. After the tour of the old school turned prison turned genocide museum we were ready for something lighter, we booked a cultural dance show. 90% of Cambodian artists were wiped out during the killings but one man made it his mission to get all the remaining artists together to revive the arts scene. I cried the whole way there. It echoed in my head that I had read somewhere there are no old people in Cambodia. I looked out of the Tuk Tuk that sped along the dusty track, flanked by cars and saw that everyone around us was middle aged. A generation of people had been wiped out in the 1970's and the population was still recovering. That night we saw an amazing show of colourful costumed dancers and ancient folklore stories acted out by beautiful agile teenagers in funny masks.

The following day we decided to visit the Killing Fields, we struggled to find the address or a tuk tuk that would take us there. Later we realised they didn't know what 'Killing Field' we meant because there were at least 150 known sites. After the Americans stopped bombing Vietnam and Cambodia in 1975, Cambodia rejoiced but just hours later; the Khmer Rouge marched into cities telling people more bombs were on the way and they should leave their homes for their own safety. It was a lie, they were led to their deaths while the brutal regime of the Khmer Rouge destroyed the empty cities, in a bid to start a new civilisation from zero. I imagined the 'Killing Fields' as a large flat field. A friend I shared a room with in Thailand years before had told me about when she visited them, the morning after taking a hallucinogenic. I knew that wouldn't be a good idea but in my mind the Killing fields were a cartoonish hallucination as I didn't get many more details from my roommate. The place was a sombre, silent, chilling in its history and feel. In Berlin I had seen pictures, diary entries and written information. Here we were walking amongst the torn clothes of murdered victims, able to pick up teeth from the ground. I pulled at a red rag in the mud, who knew if it was a scarf, top or trousers. There were fenced off areas of land around the size of a normal back garden, on the fence posts were bracelets that travellers had left as tributes, there were so many. We left a couple too. I had heard about the 'Killing Tree' which the Khmer Rouge would hit babies against to kill them, they held them by their legs and used the tree to break their skull. The tree was now covered in bracelets, the currency of love from the travellers who came here. Why did we want to see this tree? Curiosity? I'm glad I visited it, I paid my respects to the children who had lost their lives here by acquiring knowledge about the area and paying to listen to the audio that chilled me to the bone, even under the heat of the Cambodian sun. We learnt that Pol Pot, who was the leader of the genocide, never stood trial for his crimes against humanity. He died aged 98.

NEPAL

13th June 2018

"For 10 months we've had no problem using our 'Monzo' travel card to buy stuff and take money out in every country. Today our run of luck changed, as we arrived in Nepal we needed to pay $50 for our visas. We had $20 between us. Not a problem we thought as there was a cash machine. The cash machine didn't work, so we were told to go downstairs... but we needed the money for the Visa to get past security! How were we going to get to a cash machine that was in a country we had no permission to enter? Luckily the people are really nice & security very slack, so we were able to walk basically right through! We tried another cash machine which didn't accept Mastercard. Only Visa. Up shit creek without a paddle; we were rescued by a crowd of smiling Nepalese taxi drivers. With no other choice we agreed to borrow 4000 rupees from one of the drivers & for him to take us to a hotel the driver recommended. Traffic from the airport to our hotel in Kathmandu was so bad that we sat in the heat long enough to hear about the history of the Royal Family here (they were all murdered 16 years ago) plus we were approached by three different beggars apparently from India. The traffic got moving & we tried a few different cash machines with no avail. Finally, we arrived at the hotel & the room was crap. The room next door was a lovely little apartment with aircon & actual space to walk around! Luke had forgotten his pin to his Natwest Visa so I gave him my card to try despite him previously blocking one of my cards by trying the wrong pin 3 times. I went to unpack in the room we hadn't paid for, hoping for the best, finally he came back & his Monzo had finally worked! We have a

few nights here before heading to the OSHO commune!"

* * *

Food snatching Monkeys and maroon robed spiritual seekers were our company at Osho Tapoban. I had read the auto-biography of a young seeker who, against his family's wishes, ultimately set up a commune in Nepal for the controversial Indian mystic OSHO. I had taken part in Osho meditations with my Yoga teacher in Lincoln. We'd done OSHO meditations in Costa Rica as he was the 'master' of Tyohar whose vision and life's work was the creation of Pachamama itself. The medita-tions are active rather than passive, they involve rapid breath-ing, jumping and then relaxation rather than going straight into a cross legged position. The activity is said to help expend the energy of your body so your mind and body can then relax. I had read a book on Osho's beliefs and I really resonated with a lot he said although I wasn't about to dedicate my life to his worship (at this stage). What happened to us at Osho Tapoban almost led us to renounce what was left of our worldly pos-sessions (namely: our identity) and take on a spiritual name in a ceremony called Sannyasin. We enquired about this at Pa-chamama but because we were guests for only a few weeks it would have been a bit ingenuine to rush into it and at that stage we weren't ready to let go of 'Luke & Becca'. We explored our feelings around what it would mean to change our names, I felt like it would be the final thing to 'let go', I imagined what it would mean for my well being to not carry around the burdens of the identity of Rebecca Victoria Brittain. I felt though that I had a responsibility to honour the name my Mum gave me and I felt guilty that I was considering giving it up. But I no longer wanted guilt to influence my decisions. Could I successfully live in the moment if I was 'born again' with a new identity and let the history go? The truth was I loved my name! I was connected positively to my identity and my family. To start again seemed meaningless and selfish but I could also see that holding onto an identity, grasping the ownership of a name, rather than giving it up for a new one wasn't as spiritual as rebirthing myself anew.

Osho created a programme called 'Neo Vipassana' neo = New and Vipassana translates from Sanskrit to: see things as they really are. We were to join the 'new seeing things as they really are' course at Osho Tapoban starting the following day. From what I understood, it was a daily sitting meditation which originally led the Buddha to enlightenment. I wanted to be enlightened, I wanted to be happier, live my life without stress and with more appreciation, this was perfect. For as long as I can remember I looked forward to wearing the maroon robe I'd seen monks wearing on the streets of Thailand. All Thai teenage boys have to 'do a year' of living as a monk. I'd read a great book called 'cave in the snow' about a woman who wanted to achieve the same level of enlightenment as the Buddha and had lived in a remote Himalayan cave for 9 years. I was inspired to try something similar to see the results. Our accommodation was luxurious and the food was incredible so it turned out the 'seekers life' here wasn't as basic as I assumed it would be, then again, it wasn't an ashram it was a commune, maybe that was the difference.

A Tibetan centre we stayed in in Scotland had separated Luke and I into different buildings during our stay but here we shared our apartment. I was beginning to appreciate the difference between different cultures, OSHO didn't identify as a Buddhist yet he extolled the benefits of meditation, mindfulness, love, celebration and courage. The food hall was surrounded by wild monkeys, with people in charge of scaring the monkeys away. The owners of the commune had decided that the monkeys had become too reliant on the kitchen and they should go back into the forest to search for some fruit trees. It was a difficult situation, seeing them hungry but knowing that they were wild animals that needed to stay wild. The inside of the restaurant got quite crowded, outside looked appealing to all of us, but you only ate outside once during your retreat because in a flash; your chapati would be gone to a monkey before you could say Dahl Baht! For entertainment one day after lunch I sat outside to watch the monkeys play havoc. Unfortunately, for two poor unwitting diners, who just wanted to enjoy their lunch with a view of the jungle, my 'entertainment' appeared. I felt so bad watching a gentle faced man carry his tray casually with one hand behind a lady in a maroon dress, a big hungry monkey jumped down from the roof straight onto the tray spilling curry and milk drink all over the woman's back. I knew it was going to happen, that's why I sat opposite the table outside, but when it did, I didn't laugh I just felt bad I didn't pre-warn them. A lesson in compassion needed.

The twice daily silent meditations were difficult for me, I couldn't stay awake. There were 14 of us in the warm room with just enough space on the mismatched sofas, cushions and chairs to be seated without touching each other. Our task was to sit with our eyes closed and focus on our breath. The group leaders' job was to wake people up who began to snooze by tapping them on the head with a long bamboo! When I wasn't being tapped awake myself, I snuck a look at other people getting woken up. Every hour or so we had a break to walk about or have lunch, we left in silence with appreciation of movement at being free from that room. Although I didn't feel ecstatically enlightened after a few days, I did begin to appreciate the small things around me more. I began to notice the strange little bugs on the plants, I noticed amongst the greenery some mint plants which smelled delicious. I could really feel the ground beneath my bare feet, the warmth of the earth, how amazing it felt to be outside in the fresh air after feeling sleepy and struggling to concentrate. My brain slowed down. I appreciated the beauty, smells and feel of the jungle in which we resided. In Pachamama after our body cleanse and spending some time walking around barefoot in the forest without the internet to distract me a change had happened in my perception. I felt connected to the earth if only for a second, I felt that I was witness to something incredible in the energy of the birds and the trees which were made of the same energy as I am. The trees were reaching out to me as I sat amongst them. 37 days in a forest had transported me, this Neo -Vipassana was taking me to the same place but I was still too afraid to let go fully, afraid and unsure. I knew I wanted to feel peace but it was hard work, it was so much easier to go on my phone, be distracted, unconnected to the earth, I knew, as I've known for years, that an hour a day of meditation would improve my life. We said we would do it together once we got home. People were on their phones as soon as they came out of the meditation or yoga classes. I wish I didn't have to go onto social media, but it was how I earnt money. No Facebook, no money! I wondered how free I'd feel without that. After the retreat we considered staying on a few extra days and taking Sannyasin, the cost of the room and lack of wifi stopped us which really said a lot about our commitment to becoming a disciple of Osho! Since being at the commune I've read every book I could about Osho and his talks. Unfortunately, I got the impression from one of his talks that he was homophobic. If it wasn't for that one sentence I read I might still be in the robes now, with a picture of Osho and Mala beads around my neck. I'm sure if I read more on Osho I may find his support for gay people but I hadn't at the time.

Away from the monkey's and marooned meditators we found a whole apartment for really cheap. On the way there in a taxi the host was riding next to us on a bike as we approached the property. We waved from the back seat feeling really welcome in this unfamiliar shanti town of busy dusty lanes they called streets. The journey had been quite treacherous, the commune was on top of a mountain, and driving back along high roads with no barriers scared me. In England there are a lot of rules like; wear your seat belt, get an MOT, build a road, but Nepal seemed lawless in terms of motoring. It was as if Nepal had cars but the country wasn't ready for them. The house we arrived at had beautiful wooden carved gates. Rama; our host, was a tour guide for walks to Tibet, and his wife was a housewife, they had two incredibly cute children, a girl and a little boy. We were lucky to find them. They invited us for a home-cooked tea that night and every night we stayed. I sang some English songs with Kushi, their little daughter. The house was surrounded by corn fields and other new properties, within a maze of roads with no names. Ever the adventurers we decide to take a walk out for lunch, Rama had said in the description on his online listing that 'town' was close by, we actually thought that the apartment was in Kathmandu where we spent a few days acclimatizing before we donned our robes at Osho's place but in reality we had no idea where we were. Our walk into town took over an hour and it was like walking in a warzone. Half built buildings, shanti homes, wild chickens roaming around. We were in the middle of nowhere in streets that were still recovering from a big earthquake in 2015. (The Nepal earthquake killed nearly 9,000 people and injured nearly 22,000.) (Google)

I had assumed that as the home of the world's tallest mountain, Everest, we would be able to see the mountain range but I never got a glimpse of it. It turns out Nepal is vast, being from a tiny country gave me a false sense that other countries were small too. They are not. We decided to go looking for the big mountains.

THE TREKKING

25 June 2018: B:

"I'm thinking I'll have no trouble trekking the Himalayas as I did tough mudder 4 years ago lol."

26 June 2018: B:

"2 hours and £125 later we've extended our Nepal Visa for another 15 days and bought our trekking permits. We are going to trek around the base of the Himalayas for 10 days. Luke has a detailed guide for the Annapurna sanctuary so we're on our way there by taxi now. Apparently, there is little snow so no risk of avalanche and WiFi will be hit and miss. Fear and doubts aside I'm sure this will experience the most beautiful sights...We just have to look out for landslides."

30th June 2018: B:

After 4 days in the mountains (with very little visibility through the clouds) we're thankfully on our way back to civilisation. We planned to be trekking for 12 days, but due to rain and poor visibility we've cut it short.

After trekking 33.3 miles since Tuesday we've not yet even had a warm shower! ... the moral of the story being... don't trek Nepal in the Monsoon season.

The day we set out on our Himalayan adventure we were scared yet optimistic, personally I wanted to trek the Annapurna range for years after hearing how mesmerising it was. Luke – up for any challenge, planned our route and sourced all our gear - but we were still underprepared. Our lack of forward planning hadn't really affected us until now as miraculously the weather had always been ok despite us never checking the forecast. We would check the forecast in the future for treks which require visibility. I'm not a fan of up-hill walking at the best of times but when you're piss wet through, covered in leeches which may or may not be poisoning you as you trek by mountains you cannot see – my zest for trekking ebbed away and we decided to turn back. We had a real adventure in those mountains, alone for 95% of the time, only passing people on a rare occasion. We believed that trekking without a guide was do-able and to be fair the lack of a guide wasn't the reason we gave up before the peak we were heading toward. We only got lost once or twice! The biggest threats to our safety were wild tigers and bears. We had left town straight after gaining our visa extension, we got a taxi to the end of a long dirt road we were told was the start of the trail and enjoyed a delicious Nepalese lunch. We sat outside near a chained-up dog and some roaming chickens, enjoying the company of the hosts who chatted and made us a leech repellent from salt which they tied in a small piece of cloth.

PHEDI TO DHAMPUS

We had no idea what we were letting ourselves in for. The first part of the journey was a hike up a massive rocky flight of steps, the effort to make this hill path must have been monumental, the ground beneath our feet was black slate-like stone, it was carved from natural rock. It was intense and a good introduction to getting our legs working for the rest of the up-hill journey. We walked through rice crops where Nepalese people worked around wooden shack houses. We saw some of the most incredibly beautiful views imaginable of vast green landscapes.. At the top of our first steep trek we came to what would be our first tea-house. Seeing a sign for a place to stay after the steepest climb ever was a relief. I didn't allow myself to get too excited as I know what Luke is like for choosing somewhere: picky! Luckily there were no other places to pick from. I had reserved some energy for walking past but thankfully we sat down and ordered tea and chocolate bars, despite the price being more than double what it was at the bottom of the stone stairs. We got chatting to the young guy who served us, it was his dad's place, he showed us around his rainforest 'garden' and we met two giant yaks who provided their milk. We settled into a basic room which was a stone structure with a simple bed and floral sheet. Anything would have done though and the promise of running water was a bonus. Later that evening, in pitch black aside from the candlelight, the young man's father told us about the pets he had lost to predators. He had seen a wild tiger in recent years, he wouldn't go into detail but I got the impression he was terrified at the time. He spoke of the beauty and harshness of the place, the remoteness and how he wished to be somewhere else after spending his life here. The view from this home was incredible and aside from the puppy eating tigers, it could be an amazing retreat. Living here full time would have its drawbacks I agreed, I imagined having to walk all those steps just for a trip into town. It was unreal what these village people had to live with. It made me feel grateful for the ease of living in the western world. We left early the next morning to walk up a little further and saw that there were a cluster of more homestays. We could have compared prices yesterday but we had a good experience with the family, we soldiered on.

DHAMPUS – POTANA

We were on the Mardi-Himal trekking route, the day before there was beautiful sunshine but now the rain was coming down. We were singing loudly to each other to ward off any large hungry animals. Disconcertingly we kept seeing a poster of a missing woman. We let our minds wander over what could have happened to her and could the same happen to us? She may have been eaten, fallen off a cliff or kidnapped.

POTANA – PITAM DEURALI

We pushed on after a lunch stop to get our passes stamped in a small stone hut and headed towards our bed for the night. We walked and walked and walked a little more, slowly realising we were lost; we should have seen a town by now according to our calculations. There's only one thing worse than being knackered and walking for me; walking when you know you're going to have to turn back! We somehow figured out that we must have passed our stop, we trekked back about 45 minutes and finally spotted some colourful prayer flags. We found our beds for the night, it looked like we were the only guests - the out of season trekkers! We were cold, the temperature had really dropped and in wet clothes we were struggling to get warm. We stripped off, dressing in every warm item we could find and headed out to look at the menu. One great thing about this trek was the food. If the food was bad, I'd have given up long before I did. The tea-house staff were some of the best chefs on earth. The apple pie was literally to die for, it is possible of course that the food tasted so good because we were cold, wet, tired and hungry and the pies hot and sweet – mmm I could literally trek up there now for a meal! The next morning, we were woken abruptly by the host shouting something, I opened the blinds to see the most beautiful view of my life – the Annapurna range. Wow. This view was worth everything. The clouds had cleared and the snow-capped peaks were God-like. I knew now why people did this trek, why I wanted so badly to do this despite me hating most aspects of it. The view was phenomenal. Unfortunately, view-wise that was about it for us. After another couple of days uphill, averaging about 8 miles a day we called it a day. We had made it to Forest Camp, Low camp then High Camp 2,550 metres high in the sky. Undoubtedly Luke could have carried onto the base camp of Mardi Himal 4500 metres and then onto the peak but I was done.

JEEP RIDE FROM HELL

3 July 2018: B:

I thought the ride down the hill would be a little bumpy. 'A little bumpy' turned out to be very optimistic. The Jeep service we'd heard about as we stopped for another delicious Nepalese lunch sounded like a saving grace, we would trek down-hill for 3 hours, stay at another teahouse and in the morning get a lift, in a jeep to Pokhara, the nearest town. We arrived at our overnight accommodation and despite them having no Wi-Fi, no hot water, any electricity or the other half of the bathroom sink, it was better than the night before where there had been mice in the room and no running water! Seeing a jeep from the top of the hill as we jarred our knees on the steep incline of a 20,000 step long 'rockery' was our first sign of civilization. We were so happy to be heading back after an unrewarding, 33-mile hike. We'd seen only clouds and rain apart from that one morning we'd had a glimpse of the range. In hindsight we should have headed back downhill after that, our third night, all we gained from trekking up was more wet clothes, more leech bites, and increasingly dire accommodation.

Let's get this show on the 'road'. The jeep was due to leave at 8am but 'Nepalese time' was at play; our driver was still cleaning his teeth, so we waited with a fresh mint tea. It was raining and we were huddled on the stairs making the most of using our rental jackets by standing outside. Six young guys who had been trekking the same route as us were coming for the lift downhill which meant that 9 of us were in a 5 seater, our bags and half of them were in the boot. Graciously they said we could have the front 2 seats, which was a seat and a half at best. We paid £32 for our crap room, amazing food and this jeep journey. Quite expensive for Nepal but we would be back in town and the possibility of a warm or dare I say hot shower was so appealing.

The trouble began as we exited the gate of the 'hotel' a family of three were waiting to join us. "There's no way they will fit in here" said Luke. They somehow got in. One of the young guys had to sit on the lap of the other two while a Nepalese woman and her child sat directly behind me. Her husband I assume was in the boot with the bags. This was the first of many people waiting for us to pick them up, as we came to realise this was more of a bus service than a private taxi. By the time we'd negotiated the first couple of bends there were people on the roof rack.

To set the scene on the condition of roads...

A week prior, on the way from Kathmandu to Pokhara, (the last town you see before you trek) we expected our journey to take 6 hours, it took 12 and in that time we never saw actual tarmacked road, just dirt and gravel, traffic jams, landslides and smashed up buses. We agreed we would definitely fly the return journey. The condition of this 'track' we were taking down the mountainside was perilous. One false move and we would have been rolling down the side of the mountain. I was screaming at every turn. I could see out the front window and side but each time we turned I couldn't see the road beneath us, only the possibility of death. Every few metres there had been a landslide, huge boulders had crashed through bringing giant trees down with them, what if one were to roll out and hit us? On top of that I was wiping the condensation from the windows inside! I'm not usually anxious, I've faced many fears, I've jumped out of a plane with a smile on my face, ridden a tuk-tuk in India, shaved my head. Today was not a good day for fearlessness. I was terrified of dying. This situation was so insanely dangerous I had to get out of this jeep! I thought I'd have to just walk, although it would take 6.5 hours to town. The previous night, I'd vowed never to walk again due to the hike being so tough.

Today I was willing to walk day and night to get away from this certain death. The driver had obviously driven this road many times before, but as he attempted a 3 point turn and reversed on a hill pointing us toward a sheer drop I started to wonder how could he possibly predict when anymore of this land will just slide away. He achieved this maneuver thankfully, but Luke had to sit now with his legs wide apart to make room for the gear stick! A laugh a minute. Next, the bottom of the car was scraped on one of the rocks in the road and some people shouted from behind for us to stop as he'd left part of the car behind. Thank God it wasn't the brakes; just the steps to get into this death trap. That was it for me really, I was convinced that we were going over the edge. We stopped so he could pick up steps from the roadside and to collect yet more people who wanted to get on, so I got out. As I did, another jeep miraculously overtook us with about 5-6 people on the roof rack, all screaming and holding on for their lives like a fairground ride, but this was no fun for me. "It's ok there is a woman with her child in there." Luke tried to justify why we should carry on. "This is not ok, it's really not safe." I said as I got my bag out of the back. Some of the lads had got out too and they were trying to convince me it was ok. There was no way I was getting back in. "There were people on the top! It's ok!" For me that just shows HOW dangerous it is. Where in the world would people ride on top of a jeep, on sheer, crumbling cliff edges? oh Nepal. Suddenly I realised how far from sense I had travelled. All these people are mad and suicidal. I'm the only sane one and I look like the mad one. Let them all fly off the edge. I will not follow the crowd. Luke further tried to justify that we'd paid the money, so we had to take the lift. £32 for our lives seemed a very cheap price. Convincing Luke to lose money is an absolute impossibility. By this point I was hysterical. I was crying, convinced that if I got back into that jeep, we'd all be dead. Luke then started to explain that 'the moral of the story' (eyeroll) was don't come travelling with your girlfriend. I think he was just trying to save face around the crowd that had gathered to watch us discuss being stranded on the side of a cliff. I started to walk, I didn't care how long it would take (in my 90p plastic sandals) I would have my life. Luke got his bag and reluctantly joined me, I promised I would cover the money he'd lost. As I turned the first corner two very large Rottweilers were coming towards me, they started growling. My choices at this stage were get back in or get mauled. I weighed them up carefully. I had to carefully turn back towards the crowd being mindful that turning my back on these dogs could cause them to attack. By this time a queue of traffic had formed and the vehicle behind ours looked marginally safer. The tires were thick and there were a third less people onboard. Because of the imminent dog attack I'd completely broken-down sobbing and I could hear the driver of the new jeep saying 'I'm so sorry get in'. I think Luke had been asking him to take us because our vehicle was so overloaded. I was still terrified the road would fall away beneath us, but I'd decided that's the way I'd rather go over a dog attack: less drawn out and rabid. We came to cross a giant cascading waterfall and as I cried and ironically hung on to the Jeep's roof handle, a lovely lady who was in the front held onto my arm while the driver was shouting 'Relax please, Relax please', I was far from relaxed.

After a minute or so on the road, we encountered the jeep we'd left waiting behind a John Deere tractor & trailer which was precariously hanging over the edge, I felt my premonitions had been right and people had died. I have no idea if I was right, there were flowers on the tractor & it looked like it had been knocked by a 15ft boulder which had recently ended a journey nearby. I got out again and had a wild wee round the corner – feeling like my body was evacuating anything it didn't need to survive. Now our new driver received a phone call that two more people wanted to be picked up so he was going BACK UP the mountain! Our options were to go back up (NEVER GOING TO HAPPEN) or walk for half an hour as the new driver said he would come back for us, although we'd not bought our ticket with him. We armed ourselves with a walking stick each (for fighting wild dogs) and got on our way.

We passed a few of the most remote and poor villages imaginable and saw some of the most beautiful valley & rice field views of our trip. I felt very lucky to be alive and didn't mind that I was ankle deep in buffalo shit or ice-cold glacial spring water. I'd just experienced my fear threshold. Luke was happy that we'd be getting our 10,000 daily steps! We even managed a laugh. I'd decided I was never going on an adventure again and instead would work 9-5 in a dull job, have my dinner on the table for 6 and take up knitting. My life from now on would be safe, secure and predictable. After an hour, the jeep returned, claiming the hotel where we'd bought our jeep ticket from would not give any money for our lift. Fortunately, Luke convinced him to let us on. We would get that hot shower today after all.

My feet and legs were really itchy, I thought it was just a mosquito bite and I would deal with it later. I looked down to see the biggest fattest leech, full of my blood with blood pouring out of my ankle into my shoe. I screamed again as it wriggled free. I grabbed the slippery bloodsucker and threw it out of the window. By this time, we were through the worst of the journey & the mood had lightened. The driver, seeing that I had stopped having a breakdown, started asking us for money. We had to pay him 1000 rupees after paying 3000 for the first jeep that we'd left. After a few broken phone calls to our host who put us in the death wagon it was clear he was not going to pass our money onto this new driver. Luke vowed to leave him a 1-star trip advisor review each month using different accounts! Really though it wasn't the host's fault, the roads & cars are dangerous in the mountains of Nepal, the people are doing the best they can with the hand they've been dealt. The moral of the story is... you'll always get a good Dahl Baht regardless.

* * *

INDIA

I was looking forward to showing Luke India. I had been on an organised tour with STA travel a few months before Luke and I met. About 16 of us travelled together, single girls from the UK, two couples from Canada and two couples from Australia. We were taken by every mode of transport possible from Delhi to Goa via Rajasthan, Jaipur & Pushkar. That was a trip of a life-time. We even had time to spend an afternoon exploring Agra fort and the Taj Mahal. We had a tour guide from Delhi but this time around Luke and I had only our will to get us around India and from day one it wasn't really working out.

In every country we visited we bought a sim card on arrival. In the UK for example, you can just pick up a pay and go sim from the checkout. In India this is the hardest possible task for humankind. It was soul destroying. Numerous places we tried said no, those that didn't say no wanted all the names of your family, your address in India, a passport photograph and for you to stay in a phone shop no bigger than a toilet cubicle for hours on end debating through 20 pages of a contract. It was ludicrous, Luke lost the will to live many times. I must have been at a good stage in my menstrual cycle as I was managing to stay calm and see the funny side. I had been here before, so I was used to the medieval streets and constant crowds of people but for Luke, India was all new, it took him a while to see the good parts. We planned to see Varanasi as my Canadian friends had told me they had seen a dog chewing a human arm there. Varanasi is where the Hindus burn their dead on pyres by the Ganges so I imagined we would see all sorts. We did. Seeing a child no older than 4 in his dad's arms, dead, wrapped in a muslin cloth, wet from being dipped in the Ganges river will never leave my mind. That child was alive a few days before. I realised then that the arm that I had used as an anecdotal reason for visiting here was a real person. It really hit me when I started to see all the bodies. There are over 300 taken to just two burning 'Ghats' each day.

Varanasi, the 5000 year old Holy City and the Spiritual Centre of India, is intense, confronting, beautiful and sad. I forgot how India was busy, hot, a hassle with shit and animals everywhere. I didn't forget the beauty of the Saris, the flowers, ancient Hindu traditions, the sunsets and how grateful for my standard of living it made me feel when I had returned back to England. In Nepal they said that India is an acronym for **I**'m **N**ever **D**oing **I**t **A**gain. I'm here for a second time but I can relate, it's not a place to be taken lightly. Our short, sweet chapter of solid pooing has come to a queasy end. It's also hotter than death-valley. Our tour guide keeps touching Luke which is making us both uncomfortable. Plus, he's not that great of a tour guide, constantly on his phone and not telling us much compared to other guides we've heard around us. I'm happy to take it all in regardless. The Ganges looks a little different than I expected, green instead of brown and the water is quite low because of the season.

I came hoping to get a glimpse of a dog eating an arm but instead I've saw a whole body floating in the water. within an hour of being out of the hotel. I underestimated the depth of meaning to this place. We thought the floating body was tied to a boat, waiting to be taken somewhere later but our pervy guide says that he should have had a rock tied to him to sink him to be bottom. The burning of the bodies happens at one of only two Ghats, (Crematoriums) along the Ganges, but not for children under ten or pregnant women as the burning is for purification purposes and children are still pure. Muslims and 'white people' are not burnt there either. Ashes are scattered in the Ganges while people and dogs wash and swim in the shores, the depths are full of bodies tied to rocks, 200 people a day are brought here, I wonder if the bodies get washed up downstream. How long does it take a body to decompose in water? Are Hindus better than us at dealing with death because their traditions are so strong? Within 6 hours of someone dying they are here in Varanasi to give their body to 'Mother Ganga' and their spirit is heading up to heaven by the smoke. Luke asks me to remind him what the INDIA acronym is and he says he'll definitely do Nepal again! I tell him my secret of noticing one thing beautiful for every one thing bad. While dodging horse, cow, human and dog waste down a cramped alleyway a young and smiling spiritual seeker hands me some Shiva flower offerings which smell divine. Perhaps the silver lining of my dodgy stomach is that it will help me with my bridesmaid's diet. I would be going back to the UK the following month for my friend's wedding.

I felt our Ganges sunrise tour lacked information and drama, so I insisted we go back to the ancient burning Ghat after dark on our last night in Varanasi. An adventure as terrifying as it was informative. As we walked through the dingiest and darkest riverside underpasses you can imagine we somehow arrived at the Ghat with our life and possessions intact. Adamant as I was about this adventure, I had second thoughts as we finally arrived. A family was about to burn their relative, lots of young men were coming out of the shadows saying; 'don't take pictures.' As is usual in India we were the only tourists; I felt scared. The sight of this ancient crematorium takes you back in time and I felt lost among a tradition so strange. Just as we were going to turn back a young man came over and said he worked at the Hospice behind the burning Ghat; already he had given more information than gropey guide. There is a hospice behind a 3500-year-old crematorium on the Ganges. People come here to die, they're not only brought here after death. I imagined people thinking they are on death's door making their final journey to live out the rest of their days breathing in the smoky sandalwood air. Our young guide said he 'didn't want any money', in

India this is code for 'definitely wanting money' but it was re-assuring at that moment. He said it was ok if we went closer to the ceremony, he "understood we were curious and here to learn". We were taken to the body, draped in red, a woman, the family around the body had to be her children and close rela-tives, no one was crying, no other women were there either. You're not allowed to cry at the Ghats, crying is done at home. The women stay at home because, from what I can gather one woman threw herself on the pyre of her husband, this may just be a romantic Indian tale, but that made me the only live woman at the Ghats that night. We both felt honoured to have been made so welcome by the family, they didn't even give a second glance at us; tourists, at a funeral. I wondered for the hundredth time that year if I would be so tolerant of this in re-verse. I had gatecrashed stages in Asia to sing with live bands, been welcomed into homes, given food and money for little if nothing in return, now we were at this sacred event and we were welcome. Humbled, I vowed to be more generous and open. It takes 75lbs of Sandalwood & mango to burn a body, that wood costs about $10. Some people don't have the money, so they rely on donations. According to our enthusiastic hospice worker guide the gold from jewellery and fillings is collected after the body is burned and taken to be sold in the city. This money is then donated to the Ghat to pay for the wood for the people who would otherwise not be able to afford to pay. We were shown the scales used to weigh the wood, they really were medieval. It's hard to describe the sight of the scales used to weigh the exact amount of wood needed to burn a human and how it felt to hear that women's hip bones don't fully burn so they are chucked in the Ganges, can you imagine a river full of fe-male pelvis? I feel fascinated, shocked, and disgusted all at the same time while looking at a human body burn on a large pyre. There were 5 fires burning, one for each caste (hierarchy of soci-ety) at different heights, we were shown a separate area for gov-ernment officials. All fires are lit from embers which have been burning for 3 and a half millennia. We were able to go right up to the fire, our guide said a prayer for us and smudged ashes onto our foreheads. The ashes were so black and gritty. We couldn't have gotten any closer to the Ghats unless we were being burned ourselves. Despite our educational trip Luke vows never to come back, I said maybe I'll request to be burnt here so he'll have to but honestly, I wouldn't put my family through it. Luke tipped the guide and we left pronto.

❊ ❊ ❊

10 July 2018: B:

"I'd really like a train trip - I love to sightsee whilst seated! We're going to nip to the train station later (which hopefully won't be a massive mission! Luke says after the football is over then he's at my 'beck and call'. We'll see what destinations are available to us at the ticket office! Pune would be cool as we can go to Osho's India ashram but we're open to anywhere. Hope there are seats left in the aircon carriages... in India there are 8 classes, the bottom class there are no seats, the 7th class you get a plastic stall & so on until you get an actual reclining seat in first class!"

12 July 2018: B:

"We're in bed eating just toast and soda, no energy, no trip to the train station. Just recovering from Delhi Belly."

13 July 2018

"Takes 90 minutes to buy 2 tickets, we are still unsure what we actually have. A guy waiting after us congratulated us and said that it would have taken much longer in a bigger city. A letter to the train director that had to be written despite having already booked the tickets. Now dreading Mumbai where we have to change trains for Pune."

14 July 2018

"It's a bit cramped in FIRST CLASS with a large Indian family sharing our cabin, Luke and I are sharing one seat and currently there is also another man sitting next to him. After a little altercation with a man yelling and trying to pull Luke out of the seat opposite we're actually smiling now. We have a window seat, (to share) at the moment. Luke went straight to the directors office this morning while I argued with the woman who sold us the tickets and the man who wrote the letter. Luke was offered a refund for 1 ticket but that meant we would still be £45 down if we decided not to travel. The station director (wearing a badly fitted suit and white trainers) led us across the platform while people were launching themselves at the moving train. The adventure begins. I've wanted to travel by train across India for years ... I forget why now... but this is how India is so we just have to go with it. We should probably make up with these people we're sharing a cabin with for the next 28 hours! Our new friends Needi and Moopole shared their lunch with us, gorgeous homemade, vegetarian curry, rice and chapati with a sweet dessert (a speciality in Varanasi) with an after dinner mint to finish. We even have cups for our mineral water. A lovely picnic made by their family and generously shared with us. It's very quiet, cool and the track is smooth (it is British made!). Quite unlike Thailand which is more like a badly made wooden roller coaster at the end of Clacton pier. I've not yet checked the toilets, this trip is sponsored by Imodium."

15 July 2018

"We have a seat EACH on the bus from Mumbai to Pune! With THE best invention... a divider!! Although Luke's sharp elbow has still found a route over to my side. We are heading to Pune to visit OSHO's international ashram... we need to meditate again after all this travelling!"

16 July 2018

"If we don't laugh we'd cry. Rain, rain and more rain plus an idiot tuk tuk driver who drove us to the end of a long line of gridlocked traffic in the opposite direction of our Airbnb. 30 minutes more rain walking back while he kept stopping and asking us for money. Got back soaked only to be greeted with the host who wants us to fill in a 5th bit of complex paperwork in less than 24 hours. THANK GOD & THE HOLY BUDDHA FOR RUM."

17 July 2018

"From Kathmandu (Nepal) to Delhi to Varanasi to Mumbai to Pune... India has been a frustrating shit show from start to finish. Pune has become so unbearable that we're moving for the third time. This time Cochin (Kerala). Hopefully, they have a spa which serves food washed in clean water... we need a break. I'm stocked up with Immodium, pre & probiotic and rehydration sachets for my stomach that's been dodgy since Delhi. Gutted and depressed that our trip is ending like this. Really want to bring it back around."

18 July 2018 am

"Our last flight of the year together...maybe!?

A lovely Keralan friend & talented musician I know from Lincoln has put us in touch with his Kerala family & someone will be picking us up from the airport and putting us up for free. Things are looking up! We're travelling to Cochin, Kerala from Pune."

18 July 2018 pm

"A generous man called Arafath has bought us a night in this hotel! Hopefully we will see him again later to buy him dinner."

19 July 2018

"Thank you Luke for finding the best place on Earth to spend 6 days rejuvenating our weary travelling bones! The Reminiscence Ayurveda Yoga Retreat in Ernakulam, Kerala. **Best place to be in the rain... we were sick of the potholes and hassle of Pune.**

We're now waiting for the wild elephants to make an appearance in a clearing across the lake from our veranda. We have seen a deer. *I've just had an amazing ayurvedic oil massage, and I'm looking forward to yoga, healing foods and more treatments. We came through the dark times to the light and it is bright! Ps: I've had at least 6 full body massages in the last year and throughout Asia, Indonesia and India they have all massaged my chest! You don't get that in England."*

21 July 2018 ·

"I've had a reaction to all my treatments, today I'm freezing, my body aches and my stomach has gone bad again. Hoping it's the case of a healing crisis and not some stomach parasite!! I couldn't eat my tea, so must be something going on. Luke gave me a lovely back massage and is keeping me warm. I will miss him so much when I have to leave. He's decided to stay on in India to become a qualified Yoga instructor while I go back to England alone."

23 July 2018 ·

"I literally didn't get out of bed yesterday, Luke gave me massages on my back and head which was killing me and a therapist also came to rub an amazing Ayurvedic balm/scent into my head which worked like a healing Vix vapour rub. We've done yoga and had a lovely healthy coconut pancake breakfast steamed & served in a Banana Leaf! We're leaving here on Wednesday so we're researching accommodation near a big mall so I can get some souvenirs and hopefully we will spend some time on a houseboat as that's apparently great to do here.

Today I was put into a Victorian style cupboard/box sauna that was like the stocks people were held in. During the preceding massage I had been concerned about a possible toilet run due to my dodgy stomach. How would I get out of the locked box? Would I have time to dress in my Lungi (sari/sheet): before I had to sheet! I was naked and having a massage that I knew included my stom-

217

ach towards the end. It wasn't relaxing! Then something new happened: the cupboard that had been next to us the whole time was revealed to me as a kind of person-sized sauna. In order for my entrance, it was opened and one half of the top removed, then as I sat down into the steam the other half of the top was put back on and the cupboard doors closed! The therapist stood about 3 inches from my face the whole time, perhaps to be sure I didn't pass out or escape. I closed my eyes and made it through!"

24 July 2018 ·

"Two poisonous spiders moved into our room today so we moved out. This final nail in the coffin came after the treatments seemingly made me very ill and the Wifi stopped working because of the extreme monsoon rain. 24 hours without wifi is no good for the digital nomad so we got a taxi to the nearest town!"

✳ ✳ ✳

Raj played the drums for our Kundalini Yoga class, he played his Keralan drums from his heart and soul while we danced. After class one day Raj had told me about his hometown, about how green it was and if we were to be travelling through to let him know. Kerala has been on my 'to go to' list since I left India last time, as friends were heading there after Goa when I headed home. I had heard the food was good and that was reason enough for me. Raj arranged to have a friend meet us, we didn't know more than that. We were hoping for a place to stay but in the rush of leaving the retreat we had not organised anything, we expected to have to find somewhere for ourselves when we arrived. Raj's friend picked us up in his little white car but didn't speak much English so we just let him drive us to wherever he was taking us! We took in the sites around us, green, it reminded me a little of Goa in the way that there were roads built through the green but it's hard to judge a place when you have no idea who your driver is or where he is taking you. I found the car journey worrying and we were becoming critical of every detail rather than letting it be and enjoying what was. We looked at the sky, overcast, the streets, busy, the destination, unknown. I thought to myself I would be less critical and more open to what life was delivering if I was travelling alone but it wasn't safe for me to be on my own in india. Last time in Goa when I had a little longer to wait for my airport taxi after the others had left, I walked alone into town only to be ambushed by giant rats and a Indian man talking sexual obscenities while walking behind me. It was a big mistake for me to walk around that area of Goa and I vowed I would never visit India on my own. So without Luke this part of our trip wouldn't have happened.

We arrive, eventually, at a modern white hotel complex. We assumed (as we had no idea) that he was just giving us a lift here and at best we could get a price as locals rather than as tourists. We sat in the shiny white and glass reception while our new friend spoke to the staff, he then got his debit card out and paid for our room despite our protests. We would have taken a room at someone's house for free but having someone else actually pay their money for a room for us was too much. His debit card was the same one I had from Natwest in my 20's, not once did I use it to buy weary Indian travellers a room to stay in England. This was a kindness I had not experienced, this guy was a south Indian musician and even if he turned out to be a successful rich and famous one this was still exceptional generosity. 'Only in India' is a hashtag I follow on Instagram where you could see 1000's of people hanging off of a train carriage, but we found 'only in India' did we experience the overwhelming generosity of strangers. We shared a 3 course lunch on a train with a young couple who refused to let us pay for a Chai tea and now a man, who we really didn't know, had bought us a room and had taken time out of his day to ferry us around. Why?

We offered to take our friend out for dinner, but he was rushing to a concert and wouldn't likely be back in the time we were due to stay in Kerala. After settling into our spider-free white room, complete with air-con and TV we went to explore outside. We found a sweet shop and took our time over the pure sugar delicacies, taking some lovely looking treats back to our room. Luke wanted to change rooms but I thought it was fine, I didn't want to cause a fuss, it seemed like he always wanted to cause a fuss. Often we had to change the whole place we were staying and move on after one night because the place didn't suit him. I would just make the most of where we were. He wanted everything to be his way and to his ever-changing standards. We we arguing more about having to move on because of his wanting to rather than necessity. I was tired from travelling and arguing with him just wore me out even more.

Raj arranged for another friend David to meet us the following day as we would be staying with his Aunt & Uncle! We were nervous again about what our accommodation would be like but grateful all the same. David & his Uncle met us from the train and took us by moped to their home in a leafy suburb. Auntie, like many women in their culture, rarely left the house or had need to. She proudly showed us endless pictures of big family weddings. Uncle spoke about his travel for business to Dubai and how he would take Auntie with him occasionally making her one of the only women in the area that had left the country. We love Cochin already, the train line and carriages are only 6 months old and are so modern they have usb chargers in the wall, it's very clean compared to the rest of India. The people are lovely, smiling and friendly. David knows everyone and someone even offers some street nuts they are snacking on so we get our newspaper carton each and make our way to a mall. We go for a gorgeous vegetarian meal which tasted divine & cost about £3 total for all three meals & drinks. I got 1 food envy though as I realised I should have ordered something called a Dosa, David said we could swap with him but we thought it impolite to accept. Then all three of us got on his bike to come home, we only needed to be carrying three children to have been on par with the most people-laden bike we saw in Bali. We met David's Mum, Dad, brother & wife Anu and cute little Daughter Falon to whom I attempted to sing a Disney song, as we had nothing else to offer, and they gave us fresh bananas, banana chips & coffee. We were asked back for breakfast so it's safe to say we made the right decision to leave the retreat. It was extremely beautiful at the retreat but the hospitality we found with this family was much more comforting. David's family all live together one minute away from Aunt & Uncle!

25 July 2018: B:

David's wife made us the best breakfast we've had all year. A vegetable stew made with coconut milk which we ate Indian style with our hands! Today we are going dress shopping, handbag shopping and will be booking a houseboat. Our fab new friend and guide is making our lives so stress-free. There are floods and its rainy season so where better to head next than a boat?!

26 July 2018 ·

Two journalists recently drowned in the area we were heading to the houseboat. We've decided it's too dangerous to go there so we're heading to the hills instead. Munnar here we come, Munnar is a town in the Western Ghats mountain range and a former resort for the British Raj elite, it's surrounded by rolling hills and tea plantations. I just hope they have a white dressing gown each for us... I wanna chill!"

THE POLICE STATION

"Well what a day. One of our most eventful of nearly 12 months away, maybe it was a day of drama as a farewell send off so Becca doesn't forget me while she's gone. Yesterday we got a boat to Fort Kochi, which cost us less than a penny for 3 of us to travel on. We spent the day looking round the port town and it's many giant fishing nets, but we struggled to find a place to eat as many were shut due to the monsoon season and the worst weather they have had since 2013! Still we find a place, which is average at best compared to the breakfast meal Anu made. We hug some gigantic trees and find a tailor to make a dress from fabric Becca got in Varanasi. Plus we both bought some natural oil, which smells exactly like expensive after-shave and perfume made from pure flower oil without the added alcohol, cost us £2.

To give us the full experience, David decides we'll get a local bus back, these buses are 'Mad Max' style in their looks, with crazy mad max looking drivers and are often in accidents. As we step on the crowded bus and look to find a seat the driver puts his foot down, I fly into the back window elbow first and put a massive crack across the back screen (really not sure how I didn't put it through as it is basically smashed and hanging by a thread.)

Becca does a massive scream because of the bang, so as I walk to find a seat, wiping the blood from my hand trying to avoid any attention, two fellas collecting cash on the bus approach questioning about the smashed window, I obviously deny I've done it. Then my good friend David kicks into action and has a heated argument in Keralan. These pricks are demanding 8000 rupee (£90) or they're taking us to the *police station. David continues to argue with the fellas as the bus reaches its last stop and everyone gets off. We are denied being able to leave. I feel aggrieved but looking forward to explaining to police and feel confident with David as I really like the way he's handled himself in these arguments, a man after my own heart! Becca is shitting it and saying we're gonna die, they'll take us to a field out of town and their bosses will be there to lynch mob us! I thought I had a colourful imagination! So as we pull up at the station, David marches there with us first to get our side of the story across, followed by 3 fellas from the bus. There are lots of police at the station and we see 2 blokes handcuffed with black head masks being led away for some serious crime, still I'm fearless.*

David goes on to explain what has happened in his native Malayalam and I chip in with my 'The window was already cracked when we got on and they are trying to rip me off because I'm a white guy routine' but the star of the show is him, he not only explains and gains sympathy from the police for me, but also ensures the driver and friends a telling off. We have to give our British home details (our Dawny might get a knock!) and answer the favourite Indian question of our fathers name, then without further questions we are released without charge. It's then off to one of the few alcohol dispensaries in town, which is a small unit like a cash n carry, where all the local alchys queue at. We are there just before closing and buy brandy as a thank you for uncle Anthony and Rum and wine for us. We have to board a second mad max bus as we are not allowed on the train with alcohol. Then it's 3 on the moped for a short ride home. Back at home we wonder why Auntie Jancy seems in a mood even after we give our gifts. Becca plays them songs on the guitar and we sing and laugh about our days dramas. We later find out she took part in a march the week previous protesting about alcohol in the city. Becca goes to bed in the early hours as I stay up chatting to uncle Anthony about his Christian faith and we put the world to rights as we go through brandy and wine mixers at home until gone 4am. It's getting light out as we hug and say goodnight.

I feel so grateful to have met this beautiful Indian family and feel like they are my own... it's safe to say I'll be hanging like a basket tomorrow."

* * *

MUNNAR

The wine and spirits we bought back turned out to be a big mistake as Auntie is a passionate activist. Uncle and David loved a drink and advised Luke and I to drink and basically ignore Auntie. This was a very awkward situation made more awkward by the fact that we drank half the booze before realising she was upset that the alcohol was in her house. She stood next to us at the table the whole time saying stuff in her native language and pointing, I stopped drinking after we finished the first bottle of wine and I went to bed but Luke and Uncle then finished a bottle of Brandy. The next day Luke was as sick as a dog as we went to Munnar and we left Auntie and Uncle to mend their differences. I had lost count of the number of times Luke had thrown up out of a moving car door! Thought until now it had just been travel sickness! We were both craving chips so David took Luke to a market but thought we meant dried banana chips, eventually we went to an upmarket hotel and waited in reception for them to cook us some fries! We left the city to drive into 'God's Own Country' which was breath-taking. David had enlisted the help of his friend Benoy as a driver for us for the weekend and we negotiated a payment for both to be our tour guides. As we reached a dense jungle area I heard a most beautiful piece of music, it turned out to be meditation music with an ethereal woman singing Sanskrit – I felt I'd heard some of the words before. I'm not sure whether he chose that song intentionally but the moment was perfect, I looked out of the window at God's own country, breathed in the fresh, wet jungle air. After 5 minutes Luke had enough of the music and asked David to change it, the moment was gone but I was so grateful for it, grateful for this whole year away and glad we could spend the last days of it somewhere so beautiful. We came up to a waterfall where a young Indian man asked to have his photo taken with us, as white people we were a rare attraction. I wondered what he would say to his friends about who we were, Luke told him our names so it wouldn't be too weird for a stranger to have our picture. I had to leave for England soon but Luke had decided to stay and trek Everest base camp. We were both keen to make our time together as special as we could. I knew we could do this with little to no effort but Luke wanted to book the best place we could afford. Munnar is a beautiful place any time of year but the place we booked would have been better in warmer months. Our room was massive, with a hot tub but it was freezing and there was no sign of hot water. The bed was big and comfy though and we made the most of that!

Dinner demonstrated to us how much Luke was confusing people while ordering his food. He asked for a side of vegetables with his dinner but ended up with just the vege as his dinner. This had happened at a completely different restaurant proving (to me anyway) that he was the problem not them. I suggested that perhaps if he was going to be picky he should learn to speak Hindi.

30 July 2018: B:

One and a half sleeps until we part ways, we don't know when we'll see each other again. After all this time together it's going to be such a wrench to be apart.

31 July 2018: L:

"Sad times.... I've just got to the airport to say goodbye to my angel Becca, only to be denied entry to the international departure lounge by the military as my flight is domestic. We said our tearful farewells and I just want to remind Becca of my gratitude in sharing the best year of my life with you travelling the world

together. Happy 1 year travel and 2 year Lifetime-Lover anniversary. Feeling emotional, but looking forward to the next part of my adventure as a Lone Ranger traveller... until we meet again BB, be happy, travel safe and know that I am always with you beautiful ,I wrote you a poem..."

"Then there was you...
Others tried hard to tame me and change the man inside,
Some wanted lots of material things and
just money for the ride...

Then there was you.

There were those that couldn't empathise when
I was feeling really down, ones who said manic
Mick was their favourite type of clown...

Then there was you.

Them who deceived and were wrong right from
the start, some that took kindness for weakness
and those we broke each other's heart...

Then there was you.

You bring light to my dark, calm to my storm, rationalise
the mania and understand when I'm not on form.
Solutions to my problems and songs to make
me smile, relaxation to my stresses...
elegance to my style..."

* * *

I think back to our hike up joffre lakes in Pemberton, an adventure we only had because we were stuck there waiting to find transport for the Rockies. We were dropped off to embark on a little journey into the unknown. Horseflies painfully bit us when we stood still too long. The heat was almost unbearable but we pushed on to the first glacial lake, shaking off thoughts of anything else in the world. We bonded tightly over something we were good at, being in nature, being in wonder. Each stage had a new challenge that came with new beauty. We spotted a tent by a lake that overlooked mountains that looked to me like the best place on Earth. When we got to the peak Luke wanted to film himself crossing the white water of the raging glacial spring, the source of all the lakes we'd passed. It didn't look safe to me. I didn't want him to do it. Despite my protests I couldn't talk him out of it. I had to walk away. Leaving him to do what he needed to do. Hopefully showing him the way.

* * *

Our last challenge was being ok regardless of where we were, without one another. After 365 days travelling through light and dark we'd earnt a little time apart.

On the 2nd anniversary of our first date I flew home alone.

THANK YOU

Thank you Luke for allowing me to write about our relationship in these pages. Thank you also for persuing me on POF and for falling in love with me. Your kindness and generosity knows no bounds. I love you.

Thank you Mum for reading through this with me. Thank you Ruth Charnock for casting your eye over it and giving me some much needed pointers. Thank you Richard Thomas for the cover design.

Thank you Anna Jo for your support and encouragement.

Thank you to everyone in our Travelling Light and Dark facebook group. You followed and supported our journey from the start. I hope you enjoyed reading about it while it was happening for us.

Thank you Bali Olive for your long naps so Mummy could get this finished during Lockdown 2020!

✻ ✻ ✻

Rebecca is currently working on her next book:

Emotional Esther and Coco Wallace make a baby. (Working Title)

Printed in Great Britain
by Amazon